C000053917

GLIDING IN 8 DAYS

Adrian Morgan

GLIDING

IN 8 DAYS

OSPREY

To Rona, who let me fly

Published in 1990 by Osprey Publishing Limited
59 Grosvenor Street
London W1X 9DA

Text © Adrian Morgan 1990
Photographs © Kos, Oli Tennent, Adrian Morgan

This book is copyrighted under the Berne Convention. All rights
reserved. Apart from any fair dealing for the purpose of private
study, research, criticism or review, as permitted under the
Copyright Act, 1956, no part of this publication may be
reproduced, stored in a retrieval system, or transmitted in any
form or by any means, electronic, electrical, chemical,
mechanical, optical, photocopying, recording or otherwise,
without prior written permission. All enquiries should be
addressed to the publishers.

British Library Cataloguing in Publication Data

Morgan, Adrian
    Gliding in Eight Days. (In 8 Days).
    1. Recreations: Gliding
    I. Title   II. Series
    797.55
ISBN 0–85045–975–3

Phototypeset by Keyspools Ltd, Golborne, Lancs
Printed in Great Britain by BAS Printers Limited,
Over Wallop, Hampshire

Editor: Richard Widdows
Page layout: Melanie Clitheroe
Illustrations: Melanie Clitheroe (adapted by permission of Derek
Piggott)
Front cover: Rod Sutterby

CONTENTS

Acknowledgements

Without the help of the Booker Gliding Club and Phil Phillips, who manages the Lasham Gliding Society, this book would not have been written. Both offered a week's course enthusiastically and free of charge. I am especially grateful to my instructors Dave Byass and 'G' Dale, who patiently taught me as much as I currently know and, what's more despite my shortcomings, urged me to continue. The quotes from *The Sky Beyond*, by Sir Gordon Taylor, are courtesy of Cassell Australia (1963). Special thanks also to Koren Evans who took many of the photos in the book (though she had never set foot in a glider before) and Terry Joint, Lasham's Chief Flying Instructor. And finally to Derek Piggott, the father of the British gliding movement, who agreed to check the proofs, allowed me to quote from his books and gave me hours of his valuable time on a perfect soaring day.

INTRODUCTION

It was my grandfather who encouraged me to believe that if I strapped two bits of plywood to my arms and ran then I could fly. He would have known that by the time I had saved enough pocket-money to enquire about the price of wood, I would also have learned enough about the aerodynamic capabilities of humans to realise that the idea was fraught with problems.

Despite this early disappointment flying remained a dream, but at school I was persuaded to join the sea cadets; my grandfather may have known little about the air, but a long career in the Royal Navy saw to it that he passed on his passionate love of the sea.

Flying at school there was. I remember lazy days on the playing-fields watching the air cadets formate with arms outstretched, chorusing the flight-paths of a dozen simulated monoplanes. At least we had proper boats, we thought smugly, as the geography master informed his squadron that they had all overshot the runway, crash-landed and were probably even now picking grass out of their flying jackets.

Then, one day, we witnessed an extraordinary sight. Across the fields came a file of boys pulling a latticework of wood attached to a pair of wings and tailplane. It looked like a relic of something that might once have shot down a Rumpler over the trenches near Ypres.

It was clearly a glider – as any self-respecting schoolboy knew. That our elders and betters would actually allow anyone to fly it seemed incredible. Now, fired by those tales of escape from Colditz, I imagined myself at the controls of this contraption, wheeling over the towers of School House with my silk scarf trailing in the breeze, waving a defiant farewell to the headmaster and his staff streaming out of the masters' common-room, black gowns rippling like grounded rooks.

Alas, it was never to be. The glider, which I later discovered must have been an SG 38 Primary built just after the Second World War, had last seen true flight some ten years earlier. The closest we ever saw it come to anything approaching altitude was when Simms, a dull but adventurous lad from the lower fifth, seeing his runway blocked by a pile of pads, hopped over the boundary hedge into the middle of a Colts cricket match, scattering batsmen and fielders to the safety of the boundary.

As an escape bid it was a dismal failure, but the pilot was a hero for a term and the story, embellished with age, is probably still told on the playing-fields of that particular school. The glider, for all I know, is still in use. Of Simms I cannot say.

———

Gliding is a serious sport. As with anything that involves the distinct possibility of death or serious injury those who fly soon acquire a healthy respect not so much for the air as for the ground. Any yachtsman will tell you that it's not the open sea that holds terror but the nervous anxiety of approaching an uncharted coast with an onshore breeze. Unlike the yachtsman who can, more often than not, decide simply to turn tail and beat back to the safety of open waters, a glider pilot knows that sooner or later what has gone up will, inevitably, come down. The pilot's skill rests not only in keeping the glider up for as long as possible but also in landing it safely, not necessarily at the place from which he set out.

Anybody who has seen a glider trailer parked in a field will realise that forced landing, or 'landing out', is as much a part of gliding as catching thermals and soaring for miles across country. The glider pilot is always aware of the forces balancing his act and is consistently assessing his chances of staying up against the need to look for a suitable landing place.

In most cases this will be the airfield whence he came but, like a yachtsman forced by circumstances to make an unplanned landfall, almost any sufficiently large field that's clear of cows, cables and standing crops will do. Any pilot who has not landed out is

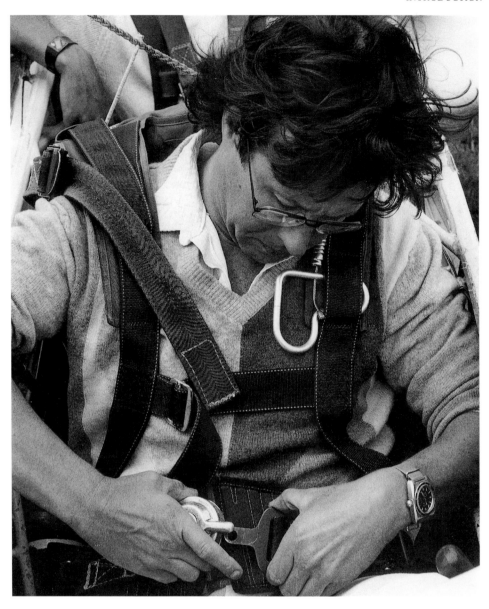

probably either a genius or not trying hard enough.

For my attempts to glide I chose two of the largest gliding centres in Europe: Booker, near High Wycombe in Buckinghamshire, and Lasham, near Alton in Hampshire. Three days at the former and five at the latter made up the vast bulk of my flying hours. The credentials of both clubs are impeccable. Not only do they occupy superb sites within easy reach of London but also offer year-round training courses. It's rare for trainees to lose more than one day's flying in five, which is the normal length of a course.

'Please fasten your seat belts.' The author, pictured immediately prior to his first flight, tries not to think too much about what is to happen next. The straps are meant to be tight, but the parachute proved unnecessary.

I could have chosen one of over 30 gliding clubs in England alone offering training courses. Only later, when I turned up at a little airfield up in the hills near Auckland in New Zealand for a day's flying, did I realise how lucky I had been. Glider pilots trained at Booker or Lasham are respected the world over. Chief flying instructors Derek Piggott, who in 36 years at Lasham virtually wrote the training manual, and Booker's former world champion Brian Spreckley both established their clubs at the forefront of the gliding movement. Piggott, who I was later to meet and fly with, is a legendary figure; through his books and inspiration he has done more than anyone to foster the sport since the war, and if one person rekindled that spark struck by my grandfather, albeit unwittingly, it was Derek Piggott. It is his books that I have used to check vital facts and, where necessary, from which I have borrowed with his kind permission.

———

I was well aware when I started flying that the chances of going solo in the time alotted were exceptionally slim. In theory an extremely co-ordinated pilot could be close to solo by the end of a week's flying; in practice it takes a minimum of 25 flights with an instructor before he's satisfied that you're safe to take £10,000 of aircraft up on your own. In an average day no more than three or four flights are possible, and indeed more than that can overload most people's learning powers.

In Australia, where the weather conditions are more settled, a student pilot can expect 20 or more flights in a week with soaring conditions to keep him up for far longer than the 15 or so minutes on a normal training flight in England. Learning times are, naturally, accelerated the longer the air-time but, no matter where you learn, only when you are fully proficient in landing and take-off as well as flying will an instructor vacate the back seat.

Gliding is essentially a self-governing sport in most countries. In order to avoid the heavy hand of official intrusion the gliding movement in Britain, for example, the British Gliding Association (BGA), is careful to maintain its safety record. Restrictions are few and there are no licences as such, but the BGA runs a national badge scheme of increasing difficulty, based on duration of flight and height gained. Airspace is allotted by the Civil Aviation Authority for each site, depending on the movements of commercial and military aircraft.

Lasham, for example, is cleared to 5,000 feet – although all gliding has to cease when, on the odd occasion, a Boeing makes a landing for overhaul at Dan Air's flight repair facility which they sublet with Lasham Gliding Society. Booker, being closer to the Heathrow flight-paths, has stricter regulations, but in two weeks of flying you're highly unlikely to see anyone in uniform other than an off-duty policeman strapping into a single-seater for an evening flight.

While accident statistics are often meaningless you're definitely safer in a glider than in a car, a boat, on foot in a busy high street or even fishing. Every year far more anglers drown or catch the tips of carbon fibre rods on high-tension cables. Yachtsmen drown themselves with depressing regularity, usually rowing home after a night in the pub. No one flies drunk. Contrary to popular opinion insurance companies put no special premium on gliding, as they do for other forms of flying.

A glance through the regular accident bulletins issued by the Civil Aviation Authority (CAA) reveals very few glider incidents. Occasionally a glider will make a heavier than usual landing and break a tail-skid or a wheel. Most accidents occur during handling on the ground, such as a wing-tip catching a car or the tail of another glider. Mid-air collision is exceptionally rare and occurs, more often than not, during competitions when anything up to 40 gliders can be circling in the same thermal. One such collision happened soon after my last flight, during the 1989 World Championships in Austria. Both gliders landed safely and no one was hurt.

Glider pilots nevertheless live with the possibility of accidents and enjoy relating accounts of hairy moments, yet very few will have pulled a ripcord for real. The freedom of the air, one of the last, is jealously guarded.

Of all the pilots with whom I've spoken – and they come in all shapes, sizes and temperaments – none would take unacceptable risks either with their own lives or the reputation of the gliding movement in general. Behind the jokes and the tall stories glider pilots, whether they're 16 or 60, seem to acquire a maturity that comes from being in complete control of their own lives, however briefly, in a way that most people never are. And more then anything else, more than the flying itself, that was the sensation I longed to experience when I set out to learn to glide in eight short days. It was also, I hasten to add, glorious fun.

DAY ONE

It was the kind of morning on which I imagined they might have fought the Battle of Britain. A light breeze shuffled puffy clouds lazily north-eastwards, an early sun was beginning to take the chill off the damp night grass, and the scene that greeted my arrival at Booker airfield could have been taken from a war film starring Kenneth More. Any moment I expected to hear the flat, uneven roar of aero-engines cough into life like heavy smokers after a bad night and see a squadron of Spitfires bounce over the fields and wheel off in the direction of France. Instead, the slender T-shape of a glider silently nosed its way beyond the boundary hedge, banked steeply and dropped like an alighting gull on to the grass a hundred yards in front of me.

Airfields are magical places. Outside the fringe of trees that surrounds Booker the roads were beginning to choke with early commuter traffic, secretaries in glass offices opened the boss's mail and yawned, schoolchildren banged desk-tops as if the din might erase the dull memory of unfinished homework. They could have been a thousand miles away.

Although I have never struck a golf ball in anger, playing truant on an airfield on a clear Monday morning in July would be a familiar feeling to any golfer who has ever delayed his week's work with a guilty call to his office.

I was also feeling anxious. Fear of the unknown is a powerful emotion, especially for someone who breaks into a sweat every time he feels the engine screaming at take-off in a Jumbo jet and senses the fuselage flex and shudder as the aircraft lumbers down the runway. A small part of my desire to fly gliders may have had something to do with cauterising this fear – a fear that I also attributed to a dislike of being a passenger in any form of transport. Perhaps when I held the controls and felt the wings clutch and finally grip the transparent air I would relax.

The final component of my anxiety was the nagging suspicion that my ego would collapse once I found myself unable to co-ordinate and balance the forces that keep a glider in flight. One reads of natural aptitude, of people who seem incapable of failure. Would those smooth turns I had witnessed that glider pilot execute as he dropped towards the field come effortlessly, or were they the result of hours of frustrating practice?

Even then I knew the answer. At best I could only hope to be an average student. At worst I imagined the quiet word from my instructor, informing me: 'Quite honestly there doesn't seem much point in going on.'

———

My thoughts on that first morning at Booker were soon interrupted by the business at hand. Beside a collection of the kind of low huts you see on the perimeter of any small airfield stands a much smarter wooden building where three nervous would-be pilots found ourselves putting names to a simple form and taking possession of a light green British Gliding Association pilot's log-book. The first page, headed 'Previous Experience on Light Gliders/Sailplanes', would remain blank. Those flights of fantasy would not count.

The three of us, two men and Fiona, looked equally worried. There was no way of telling, short of asking each of them, 'What experience have you had, then?' whether this was their first time too. Although I was curious, I didn't want to be the first to admit my total ignorance of flying. For the time being we made do with the briefest of small talk, unwilling to probe deeper for fear of giving the game away.

Our instructor was to be Dave Byass, a young glider pilot with seven years' experience. Like many instructors he taught more for love of flying than the money, but teaching was the only way he could indulge a passion for gliding that had become a lifestyle ever since he had resurrected an old glider his parents had given him many years before.

At first I mistook his attitude to be that of a man

A quite unnecessary number of eager helpers push our K13 towards the launch area with instructor Dave Byass doing the lion's share of the work at the leading edge. To push the glider anywhere else risks damage to the sensitive wing surfaces.

who regards instruction purely as a way – a necessary evil, perhaps – of earning the means to finance his own flying. I expected an older man, an eccentric with handlebar moustache, a devil-may-care approach and a ready line in anecdotes. Much later I discovered that few of them exist. Dave may have been sparing with comment on the ground but once aloft he bubbled with suppressed enthusiasm. I realise now that entrusting your skin to a bunch of complete unknowns breeds a certain wariness in all instructors, and Dave was no exception.

He had the keen, piercing eyes of a pilot: older eyes perhaps than his years warranted. Spare and economical of movement, he could have been a gamekeeper, poacher even, speaking little, fielding our slightly nervous questions with a shrug as if to say, 'Wait and see, all will be revealed in due course.' When he did speak it was as if he was talking not to us, but to himself. Like a priest with a new batch of novices, he was to be our confessor over the next week or so, and I was to hear a great deal of that quiet, assured voice in our confession box, a clear bubble of Perspex high over the Buckinghamshire countryside.

'It looks like a good day, though the cloud base could be a bit higher,' he said as we walked over to the hangar. I'd have liked to see a little less cloud. To me a perfect flying day consisted of clear sky – the kind of day, I would discover, that they call 'blue' and is generally hopeless for soaring.

Ignorance of gliding meteorology was compounded by a total lack of knowledge about the gliding movement in general. I had carefully avoided reading too much before the course in case it either put the fear of God into me or encouraged any know-it-all tendencies. I wanted to start with a clean slate, with no preconceptions.

For a start I imagined that gliding had originated in England, but in fact most gliders are German, French or Polish. Having been denied 'proper' aeroplanes by the Treaty of Versailles, which imposed the conditions of surrender after the First World War, Germany put most of its flying energy into developing gliders. Sir George Cayley (1773–1857), an Englishman, may have been the inventor of heavier-than-air flying machines, and the Wright Brothers used gliders to learn the principles of flight that led to that historic powered flight from Kittyhawk in 1903, but the Germans were responsible for most of the early work that has gradually enabled glider pilots to remain in the air almost indefinitely in the right conditions.

Our glider for the week was to be an ASK 13. Built in West Germany, they are the standard dual-seat training gliders – forgiving, solid and yet with a performance that would until relatively recently have appeared exceptional. Memories of that old SG 38 on the school playing-fields soon disappeared.

The fuselage of the ASK 13, or K 13, is constructed around a welded steel sub-frame, over which is stretched a Dacron fabric, doped and painted. The top section of the fuselage is of moulded ply. The wings rely on a strong wooden spar and a D-shaped leading edge torsion box to stop the wing twisting under load.

All togged up and ready, parachute strapped to his back and trying not to feel like a complete novice, one of Booker's hopeful pilots prepares to go where he has never gone before. The strap on the canopy stops it swinging open too far – the most common source of glider damage.

Airspeed, yaw indicator (off), altimeter, rate of climb indicator, accelerometer, compass, feet on rudder bars and nervous hand on simple joystick – these are the simple elements of flight. The placards to the pilot's right indicate the accepted loading limits and maximum permissible speeds of the K 13 in various manoeuvres. The lever to the left controls the air-brakes.

The rear of the wing, which completes the aerofoil section, is a light, ribbed structure over which Dacron is again stretched.

The Perspex bubble canopy encloses two light-weight seats, angled back at about 45°. A short stick, which controls the ailerons on the wings and elevator on the tail, rises from the floor immediately in front of the pilot, who rests his feet on rudder pedals in the nose. A simple array of dials set in a facia provides information on speed, rate of climb and altitude. Immediately beneath the pilot is a long wooden skid. Behind that sits a single, rubber-tyred wheel. At the back, under the tail, a simple skid completes the glider's undercarriage.

More damage occurs to gliders on the ground than in the air. So graceful in flight, a glider is unwieldy on the ground and at the mercy of strong winds. When they are packed tightly in a hangar it's very easy to catch a wing and damage a control surface. The slightest knock can entail expensive repairs, and in particular any damage that compromises the strength of the D-box that supports the wing is especially serious. Not without good reason do glider pilots religiously follow the daily inspection procedure that precedes any flight, the details of which Dave invited us to watch.

A great deal of close scrutiny ensued, both inside and out, before he adjudged the glider fit to fly. Then, pushing against the front of the wing nearest to the fuselage with two people lifting the tail by the two handles at the back, we wheeled 113 at a walking pace out towards the old British Airways bus that serves as the flying centre for the day's activities. Fiona, ginger-haired and freckled, held the wing-tip clear of the ground, steering our progress towards a line of gliders, their wings held down by old tyres, waiting for the tug aircraft that was to tow them to 3,200 feet.

There are basically two methods for getting a glider aloft. The simplest involves attaching it to a tow car or truck by a length of wire or rope. Powerful wire-winches are a refinement of the principle. We were to make our ascent behind a small Robin light aircraft, attached to its tail by a 200-foot length of rope ending in two small steel rings, the last of which engages in the release hook set behind a rubber fairing flap in the nose, or sometimes the belly of the glider. A yellow toggle to the pilot's left is pulled to release the tow when the correct altitude is reached. This is the aerotow.

———

A bare minimum of instruction is allowed to clog the brain of a student on his first flight. 'I believe it's better to take people up the first time with the minimum of instruction,' said Dave. 'No time to get frightened. I like them to take control on the first flight before they know anything.'

Take control? I don't know quite why, but this announcement came as something of a shock. 'Well, what do you expect'? he continued with a wry smile. 'You're here to fly.'

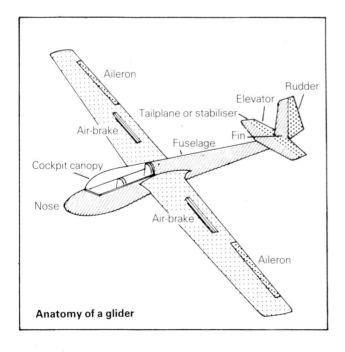

Anatomy of a glider

The K13 is the standard two-seater training glider – sturdy, forgiving and easy to fly.

Fiona holds the tow rope ring which locates in the hook under a small rubber flap in the nose of the K13. Tow ropes are continually checked for fraying and the rings inspected for damage.

Prior to his first ever flight the author considers all the reasons he can for getting out, while Dave wonders what horrors are in store for him. In the event the flight was delightfully smooth – but far too short. Note the quick release buckle on the straps and the parachute handle above it.

As we pulled 113 into line the increasing roar of an aero-engine and the smell of exhausted aviation fuel met us, signalling the third flight of the day. A glider was picking up speed. Lurching forward, leaping and bounding over the grass, wing-tips clutching at the air, it dipped momentarily towards the ground and then clawed up into the now cloudy sky. Hardly had it begun its slow upward flight than another tug dropped into land and taxied round towards us, trailing its tow rope through the short grass. I was invited to step, gingerly, into the front seat.

Some clubs, including Booker, insist on parachutes. Having never worn one, let alone deployed one, I was glad that everything was happening faster than I could assimilate. 'You won't need it,' said Dave, 'but if you do the procedure is basically to jettison the canopy by pulling this red knob, then undo straps and finally throw yourself clear. Count one . . . two . . . three, and pull the handle.'

With those comforting words still ringing in my ears I had time only to buckle my seat-belts and glance wistfully out through the clear Perspex before we too were bumping over the grass, while the stick between my legs, which I was told not to touch, jerked left and right, the pedals moving to some invisible tune played by my instructor sitting behind me.

The field stretched out for about a hundred yards ahead, dipped and then rose slightly before disappear-

The view from a passing seagull as Morgan and Byass drift over the Buckinghamshire countryside. The dark lines in mid-wing are the air-brakes which seem, from this angle, to be slightly raised. Dave was, presumably, trying to lose a little height at the time to bring the glider in line with the photographer in the tug.

ing into the trees fringing the perimeter track. Within seconds the ground was dropping away. The trees flashed by beneath as our wing-tips followed those of the tug on a gentle turn to the right. The air seemed alive, buffeted by the slipstream from the propeller, while invisible forces pushed us from below. The jerking controls were now moving more smoothly, but with an authority that I could feel surreptitiously with my thumb and forefinger lightly around the rubber grip. The glider hung by its slender rope, straining for height as I tried to relate the control movements to our attitude behind the urgent little tug.

Below our wing-tips the countryside of Buckinghamshire resolved itself into a quilt of variegated field patterns. Ahead the Chiltern Hills rolled onwards towards Oxford, and the commuter town of High Wycombe sprawled away below to our right.

As the altimeter crept towards 3,200 feet the yellow toggle on my left jerked twice and the rope sprang forward. The glider banked steeply to the right in a climbing turn that left me feeling queasy. The wing dipped sharply, the ground stared me in the face and disappeared again beneath the fuselage as Dave levelled off.

The buffeting was gone now, replaced by a smooth, almost silent swish as the glider tasted freedom. Enclosed in our bubble, with the grey base of the clouds within touching distance above us, we drifted wordlessly towards the horizon for several minutes before a voice from behind invited me to place my right hand lightly on the stick.

'Follow through with me,' it said. 'You'll find that the glider will fly itself if you let it. Try to keep the wings level by moving the stick gently. Notice that when I move the stick left or right I move the pedals at the same time. The rudder counteracts the glider's tendency to swing in the opposite direction to the bank as you move the ailerons. The object is to keep the turns smooth, with stick and rudder together.'

Every so often as we wandered about the sky the glider would come alive to disturbances caused by the last traces of weak thermals rising off the fields below. I knew that air could be troubled. Anyone who has ever watched the seat-belt sign flash on, usually during a meal, on a commercial flight will have experienced the sickening jolting as the aircraft flies through pockets of turbulence. Now we were using them to gain height.

To a glider pilot this uneasiness usually signifies rising currents of warmer air and he will be alive to their presence – as I discovered when Dave banked

Dave puts the glider into a steep left turn to bring himself over the airfield, with the perimeter track visible in the centre of the picture. The speed is a healthy 55 knots according to the airspeed indicator on the left, which suggests that he is setting up for the landing.

steeply to the left and began circling over a patch of darker fields. The altimeter, which had dropped steadily from 3,200 to 2,500 feet, was now creeping up again. A high-pitched squealing was also emanating from somewhere behind the instrument facia. 'That's the audio variometer,' explained Dave. 'It tells us whether we're in lift or sink. The higher the pitch the better the lift.' The variometer seemed to agree: its pointer, until then firmly stuck a little below horizontal, was now registering +2, a lift rate of two knots.

The glider may have been dropping but the air was rising faster. Like a man trying in vain to walk down an 'up' escalator, we were being lifted by the warmer rising air beneath us.

Too soon that first flight drew to its inevitable close. Without lift a glider, however imperceptibly, will come down. High-performance gliders may have a glide ratio of more than 45:1 – that is, for every 45 feet they travel they will sink one foot. In our K 13, with its large wings and relatively poor gliding angle, we were losing one foot for every 16 we flew. Soon the altimeter was showing 1,000 feet and the airfield, without my consciously having noticed it, had miraculously appeared about 30° below our right wing.

For a while we flew downwind, parallel to the landing area. The T-shapes of gliders and the control bus, surrounded by small figures, were clear below. Dave dropped the nose a little and the speed rose to 55 knots. The rushing sound increased as we banked sharply to the right. The landing field began to swing into view ahead and beneath us. The wings levelled. The blue lever on my left clunked backwards. To each side flat slabs of metal appeared from above and

The stick and rudder together control all the glider's movements: pitching, rolling or banking, and yawing.

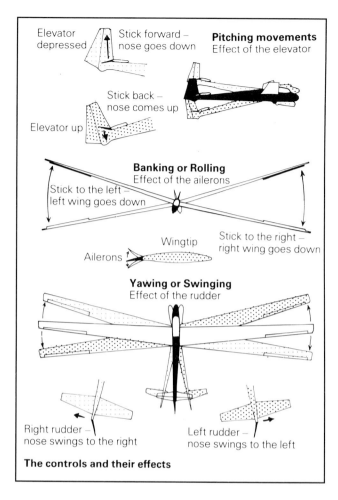

Pitching movements
Effect of the elevator

Elevator depressed

Stick forward – nose goes down

Stick back – nose comes up

Elevator up

Banking or Rolling
Effect of the ailerons

Stick to the left – left wing goes down

Stick to the right – right wing goes down

Wingtip

Ailerons

Yawing or Swinging
Effect of the rudder

Right rudder – nose swings to the right

Left rudder – nose swings to the left

The controls and their effects

below the wings. As the air-brakes bit the glider began to drop, sinking forward and down towards the grass which seemed to spring up, surrounding us in green where before all had been grey and blue.

Seated low down in the nose of a glider, like the driver of a go-kart, 55 mph feels like much more. A few feet off the ground the grass rushed by until, with a slight jolt, the tail skid touched, followed immediately by the bump of the wheel. A few more yards and the glider came forward a little on its skid, and the noise of grass brushing the steel shoe decreased. The ground began to slow its pace towards us and finally stopped as the left-hand wing tilted, then dropped gently to the grass.

Two faces peered in through the canopy. Dave shot the bolts locking in our little world and the air rushed in. Having expected nothing, it was nothing like I had expected. I think I grinned and gave the thumbs-up sign.

DAY TWO

That night I dreamed of flying. Psychiatrists can say what they like but this was the real thing, a semi-nightmare in which the stick seemed to have no corresponding effect on the wing surfaces. The more I pressed forward the more the glider climbed. The rudder pedals too had a mind of their own, jerking left and right. Only the landing was smooth. The green of the airfield invited me softly.

One of the first things that a glider pilot learns to accept is that there is a great deal of sitting around waiting to fly. In over eight hours on the airfield we had only managed two flights each. My total flying time was 34 minutes, 25 of which were during that first introductory flight from 3,200 feet. Thereafter the tug had taken us up to just half that altitude and, as the clouds began forming an impenetrable canopy above, so flight times had dropped. Any lift there had been evaporated. It was the same the next day.

Grey, windless days are not conducive to long flights. Restricted by a low ceiling of cloud and an aerotow limit of 1,600 feet we were unlikely to break any records for duration flying. In what little time was available we were to spend working on smooth turns.

Before attempting aerotows or landings students are taught to handle the glider, and in smooth air the learning progresses apace. Those first flights seem to resound to the call from behind: '*Stick and rudder together*.' It reminded me of an Austrian ski instructor in Kitzbühel: 'Bend ze nees, zo. Bend ze knees.'

Having used the stick and rudder the previous day without quite knowing exactly to what they were connected, I then had Dave spend 15 minutes explaining the control surfaces. Ailerons on the trailing edge of the wings control the angle at which the glider banks or rolls. They work by altering the wing profile, increasing the lift on one side or decreasing it on the other to create an imbalance that tips the glider in the desired direction. Dropping the right aileron – that is, moving the stick to the left – produces more lift from the right wing, which causes a bank to the left. If you've ever put a hand out of a car window at speed the effect of tilting the palm upwards will be well known. At the same time as the stick is moved to the left, the left-hand aileron hinges upwards, decreasing that wing's lift and causing the glider to take up an increasingly steep left-hand bank until the stick is centralised again.

But banking is only one component of the turn. Depressing the right aileron may provide more lift to that wing but it also increases the drag, holding the wing back in the turn. Unless a little left rudder is applied to keep the fuselage straight the effect of stick alone will cause the glider not only to bank to the left but also swing, or 'yaw', its nose to the right. This is called adverse yaw and is the effect of aileron drag. Learning to co-ordinate stick and rudder movements is thus the first of the many hurdles to be overcome.

The sequence is simple. First, the pilot scans the horizon. When turning to the left, for example, he will

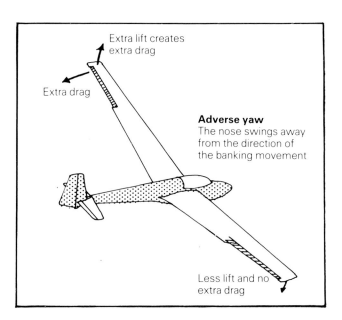

Extra lift creates
extra drag

Extra drag

Adverse yaw
The nose swings away
from the direction of
the banking movement

Less lift and no
extra drag

Aileron drag causes the nose to swing away from the turn, ie adverse yaw. The rudder controls this tendency.

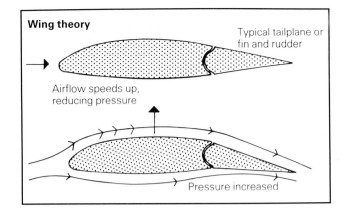

Wing theory

Typical tailplane or fin and rudder

Airflow speeds up, reducing pressure

Pressure increased

The theory of a wing, in its simplest form. The ailerons alter the profile, producing more or less lift in that wing and thus causing a bank or roll which is the major component of a turn.

pan from behind the right wing, over the nose to the left and then, facing forward again, move both stick and rudder to the left. When the angle of bank is reached the stick is brought back a little past the centre and the rudder is then eased back to stop the nose drifting too much into the turn.

When the angle of bank is set the glider will stabilise in the turn. The pilot continues to check the horizon, judging his turn by the angle the left wing-tip makes with the ground below, correcting a little if the bank becomes too shallow or increases further and balancing stick with rudder to achieve a smooth turn.

Once the pilot becomes fully aware of his surroundings he will notice above him, stuck to the outside of the canopy, a little tuft of wool. If the turn is smooth the string will fly straight back, which means that the fuselage is meeting the airflow head-on, giving minimum drag. A skidding turn, with too much rudder applied, or a slipping turn, with too little, causes extra drag as the fuselage goes sideways through the turn. Height is lost and, in the absence of lift, flight duration is cut.

The stick also controls the elevator on the tail. This makes the glider climb or dive, losing or gaining speed as it does so. In level flight the elevator is, in effect, the glider's throttle. The optimum speed varies from glider to glider: in our case the K 13 is happiest at about 45 knots. On landing the pilot will depress the nose by pushing the stick forward, thereby increasing the speed as the glider's weight falls forward more steeply towards the ground.

It's exactly like a bicycle freewheeling downhill. And just like a cyclist trying to freewheel uphill, a glider will eventually stall if the nose is kept high; the wings take up too high an angle with the air and the speed drops to below that needed to produce lift.

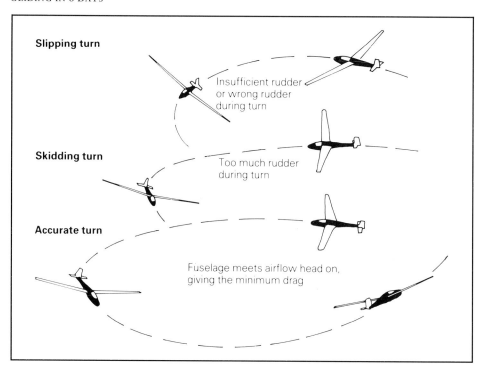

Slipping turn

Insufficient rudder or wrong rudder during turn

Skidding turn

Too much rudder during turn

Accurate turn

Fuselage meets airflow head on, giving the minimum drag

Too much or too little rudder in a turn causes the glider's fuselage either to skid or slip, which is inefficient. The fuselage, ideally, should meet the airflow nose-on.

All this is well known to anyone who has ever made model aeroplanes in his childhood. Most of mine used to crash, but that was half the fun. When you start relying on the principles of flight to stop your own carcass plunging to earth you tend to pay a little more attention.

Rudder co-ordination is the student pilot's biggest initial problem. The natural desire to jam the rudder over and expect the glider to turn without touching the stick is, at first, tempting. The correct action is not instinctive – unless, of course, you have piloted soapboxes as a kid. The need to lean into the turn as you apply foot pressure to the pedals corresponds reasonably well to the initial problems of turning a glider.

By now we were all beginning to enjoy the prospect of flight. Flight times were too short to be wasted. While waiting for our turn there was plenty of time to think about the last flight. On the ground it all seemed so straightforward: stick and rudder together, stick central, rudder back, keep the bank on, keep looking over the nose smooth and easy. At 1,500 feet and horizon spinning round it was all too easy to lose concentration. The yaw string would swing over, the sound of the airflow rushing in through the little sliding side window would tell us that we were slipping sideways, and before long that voice from the back would say quietly but firmly, '*OK, I have control.*' The words, even now, carry a sense of failure and frustration.

My fellow pilots were also feeling that sense of inadequacy. Fiona in particular was finding it hard to relate how the controls were affecting the glider's attitude in flight. Cursed by the typical British upbringing where women are seldom encouraged to understand the working niceties of mechanical objects, she was at a double disadvantage. The two men, on the other hand, knew what should be happening and were angry that it wasn't – or rather not as smoothly or effortlessly as they would have liked.

Fortunately there is always plenty to do on the ground. Every flight has to be logged, not only to enable the club to tot up flying time and charge accordingly but also as a safety requirement. Any gliders not logged back in at the end of the day are presumed to have landed out. Every so often another pilot will stroll over to the log-keeper to see how long the gliders are staying up – a sure sign of the presence or otherwise of thermals. In our case, though not entirely through our fault, that meant 'not long'.

Checking off pilots' names as they climb into the cockpit is only one of the tasks. Landing times are also logged, although the pilot is expected to make a separate note. With gliders leaving at regular intervals and others landing, not always nearby, the log-keeper

The stages in a turn begin with a good look-out followed by stick and rudder movements together until the bank is established. The stick is then centralised, the rudder eased and the glider will maintain a steady turn until the pilot wishes to regain straight and level flight, when the actions are reversed.

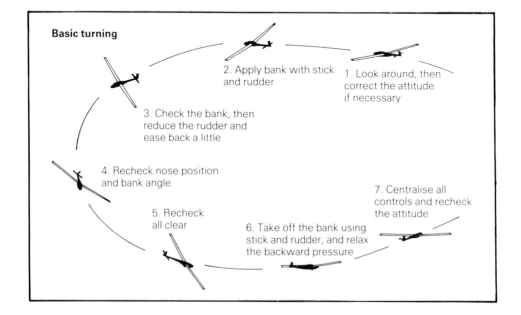

Basic turning

1. Look around, then correct the attitude if necessary

2. Apply bank with stick and rudder

3. Check the bank, then reduce the rudder and ease back a little

4. Recheck nose position and bank angle

5. Recheck all clear

6. Take off the bank using stick and rudder, and relax the backward pressure

7. Centralise all controls and recheck the attitude

has his hands full noting registration numbers, names and landing times.

He also plays a vital role in controlling the take-off procedure. At Booker the flights are almost entirely controlled by the man in charge, who relays instructions to the tug pilot via a hand-held radio. Other clubs have slightly different procedures and place more responsibility on the pilot in the glider. The first duty is to tell the tug pilot the glider pilot's name for his own log. At Lasham, for example, once the glider is in position and his pilot has completed his check it's up to him to make a careful lookout in front. He will then shout to the man holding the wing of the glider: 'Are we all clear above and behind?', accompanied by a circling movement of his hand.

Once the all-clear has been given he will then ask for the tow-line to be taken up slowly. 'Take up slack' is accompanied by a one-finger salute. Once the rope is tightened the signal 'All out,' is given; the tug accelerates away and the wing man runs with the tip until the wing generates lift, usually within a few seconds. These signals are relayed to the tug pilot either by radio or hand signals, and sometimes both.

The signals for winch tow are the same and are relayed to the winch driver by a sequence of flashing lights on the front of the control vehicle. The British Gliding association has adopted standard launching signals.

Logging flights becomes an accepted part of the waiting around. The process is vital, but there's also a certain pride to be had in getting it all down accurately – and it absolves you from retrieving gliders that land far out on the field.

———

Flight four was again brief. Four minutes on tow, bucking the Robin's wake, five minutes practising turns and two setting up for the landing. I was banking too steeply and too fast. The voice from the back was trying to get me to turn gently. 'Try to keep a steady 30° turn using stick and rudder,' it intoned. 'Always stick and rudder. The stick makes the turn, the rudder keeps the nose from swinging left or right. It's a matter of co-ordination.' It wasn't easy. I even tried leaning into the turn like on a motorbike, but it didn't help and certainly didn't feel natural.

Nevertheless, despite the first of what was to become a series of frustrations, I was beginning to enjoy the prospect of the next flight. Apart from the bumpy take-off. That, and the sense of not quite feeling in control, I could do without.

The accepted pilot's signal for 'Take up slack'. The one-fingered salute is relayed to the tug pilot who rolls forward until the tow rope is 'All out', for which the signal is two fingers. The pilot can release at any time if he is not ready. Note the small sliding window in the canopy.

Flight five lasted barely ten minutes, four of which were under tow, but basic turns were coming on well. I abandoned the idea of trying to fly the glider like a motorbike, and it seemed to help. Looking over the nose and not down at the wing in the turn was also producing an improvement. But, as always, the flight was over almost before it began.

Instructors vary but most will adopt the overlapping approach, whereby a new skill is introduced just as the pilot is beginning to master the last one. It can seem that the instructor is cramming too much too soon, but once you start concentrating on a new skill the old ones seem to resolve themselves.

In my case it was now time to take some control, at least, of the landings. Initially this seems much easier than the take-off. In common with most students I found the aerotows rather daunting without having full confidence in the controls. Although in many respects the take-off is the simplest part of the flight, there are parts of the landing that come much more naturally at first to a student.

The small trim tab on the elevator is connected to a lever in the cockpit so that it can be set in flight to balance the glider, compensating for pilot weight. It also allows the pilot to trim the glider to fly at a certain speed without further movement of the stick. The left-hand air-brake, which spoils the airflow over the wing, causing it to lose lift, can be seen fully extended.

So many new things crowd into those early flights that it's virtually impossible fully to enjoy the experience itself. For example at this stage I was only vaguely aware of height, the countryside and even where the airfield lay. Signposts as clear to a pilot as a motorway turn-off, a line of trees or a small village mean nothing to a student wrapped up in the process of co-ordinating wretched stick and rudder pedals that have a mind of their own.

It's all too easy to concentrate on smooth turns and lose track of where you are in relation to the airfield. The pilot, responding only to the voice from behind, is unaware that all the time the instructor, as well as trying to impart the rudiments of wisdom, is edging the glider back towards the circuit, mentally checking that enough height is left to enable the glider to approach the landing area safely.

Eight minutes into the fifth flight Dave took control. The airfield had miraculously appeared again to our right when he suggested I trim for 55 knots. What on earth did he mean?

To the pilot's right lies a small lever, attached in this case to the frame by a bolt and a wing-nut. With the right hand still lightly holding the stick the trimmer, which activates a small flap on the elevator, is pushed forward with the left hand. The flap or tab produces a slight download at the trailing edge of the elevator, causing an imbalance which has the immediate effect of holding the elevator down. The pilot feels this as a small forward movement on the stick. This then lowers the nose and the glider increases speed.

As the nose goes down speed continues to increase, and will do so until the glider reaches its new, trimmed, balance. Subtle adjustments to the trimmer will stabilise the speed – in this case, landing a K 13 into a gentle headwind, one of 55 knots.

Increasing the speed is one of the first rules of landing. At first this may seem strange, perhaps even dangerous, but it's essential in order to give better control in the more turbulent air near the ground and to keep the speed well above stalling point in the critical final approach.

Without that extra speed the glider pilot has no leeway. Once the glider reaches stalling speed, about 30 knots in a K 13, controls become sluggish, height falls away rapidly and the danger of a spin increases. By keeping the speed up the pilot retains control in the vital final turn towards the runway which is often fairly steep and low and can burn it off at will for the landing. The last turn is normally banked at 45°, the most efficient angle, one that loses as little height as possible for the most effective turn in a given time.

We were by now flying downwind parallel to the runway at about 500 feet. 'I still have control,' Dave said as we banked into a steep, fast turn over the trees at the end of the field. As we levelled out, our speed pinned at 55 knots and the airfield swung into view. 'OK, you have control,' he said. 'But don't worry – I'm right there. Keep the speed at 55 and the wings level. I'll do the rest.'

I grabbed the stick a little too fiercely and the nose dropped. The needle swung to 65 knots and the noise of the wind increased. 'Back on the stick a little,' came the voice. The nose lifted slightly and speed fell. The wings were dipping alternately as the glider, like a horse sensing his stable, tried to persuade its insensitive rider to relinquish control and let it land itself – which it seemed entirely capable of doing.

Once lined up for the landing the pilot must keep to the required speed. Heading steeply for the runway at 55 knots seems alarming to the novice. The ground comes up fast and, as the glider continues to move forwards over the ground, the point at which you are aiming begins to vanish beneath the nose. At this point I was again aware of the invisible hand on the air-brakes to my left and right. The aiming point began to recede. The glider, robbed of excess lift by the brakes, began to drop towards the grass. 'OK, that's fine. Now round out.'

At 20 feet the ground was coming up to meet us.

Gently easing back the stick into near level flight, the speed dropped and we floated on a cushion of air until, with a jolt, the wheel touched. 'Back with the stick. Keep the wings level. Steer with the rudder,' came Dave's voice calmly above the noise of the skid slicing through the grass beneath us.

Back with the stick? Surely we'd just leap back into the air? What the hell was going on? This didn't feel right. 'The idea isn't to drive the glider into the ground,' explained Dave patiently. 'Let it settle, like a bird. Once the speed has been scrubbed off it'll land itself – and once on the ground it'll stay there. Obviously, if you pull the stick back too high and too fast you'll start to climb. That's called ballooning, and there's a technique to stop it we'll get onto later.'

Landing, says Derek Piggott, is a more natural process than trying to synchronise stick and rudder. Well, possibly. 'Whereas everyone has a problem in learning to use the rudder correctly in conjunction with the stick movements,' he writes, 'it is unusual to have much real trouble over learning to land. Look well ahead during the final approach – 100-200 yards ahead and not just over the nose. Start levelling out with a minute backward movement on the stick at about 20-30 feet so that by the time the aircraft is flying level it is two to five feet above the ground, not too close.'

It sounded simple. The stick and rudder bit was hard, I granted, but at least there was time to think up there. The approach all happened so fast. From the ground, however, it did indeed look simple. The turn, the steep glide towards the ground, the air-brakes and

Using an aiming point

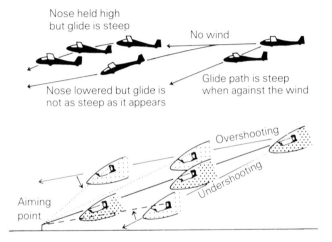

The chosen aiming point, usually a spot just beyond the perimeter track of the airfield, will recede or disappear below the nose depending on whether the glider is undershooting or overshooting. It's no more than a reference point for the pilot to judge his landing correctly.

Dave circles over the perimeter to lose height, his wing-tip pointing at the control bus where a glider is about to start its aerotow. Airspeed is just over 60 knots and the altimeter reads exactly 500 feet.

Then, levelling out at 100 feet, the glider skims the main road, heading towards the control bus at the perfect approach speed of 55 knots. There is a 15-knot crosswind blowing from right to left across the line of flight; hence the glider's attitude . . .

. . . and the result, a perfect landing by the bus.

Logging off flights as they take off and land is a job that everyone has to do at some point. It's vital not only to enable the club to charge according to flight times, but also to keep a check on who is where.

then the float into land with the aim being to let the aircraft drop gently onto the ground as the wings lose lift rather than trying to fly it down, which is a sure recipe for a heavy landing.

We had plenty of time that day to practise vicarious landings. Watching other pilots land was an excuse to air our new-found expertise. 'Oh, oh. Rounded out too soon. What a cock-up!' Points were awarded for style. We began to see how the controls affected the attitude of the glider in the turn. Too much rudder sent the glider into a skid. Bouncy landings were a source of great mirth. Anyone who managed to land within 150 yards of the bus received a silent round of applause, since it saved a long walk to retrieve them.

It had only been five flights, but it seemed like much more. Being involved with the minute-by-minute activity of a busy airfield, logging flights, retrieving and occasionally flying allows time to think, avoiding the overload that can lead to brain scramble. Watching other pilots, living their problems with controls, is all part of the learning process.

___

As I sat down on the steps of the bus to read more of Derek Piggott's section on landing, a 16-year-old girl was stepping gently into the seat of a solo K 8. Already she had completed her Silver C, which entails a flight of not less than five hours. 'It's not too hard,' she said. 'I suppose you learn quicker if you're young.'

As the tug plucked her into the air Fiona, with just one more flight than myself in her log-book, was approaching the runway. Dave was obviously talking her down gently, letting her feel the air-brakes bite, before guiding her to a good landing 200 yards from the bus. EBZ, on the other hand, came in high about ten minutes later, levelled out, rose 20 feet back into the sky and floated away down the field before coming to rest opposite the hangars a good quarter of a mile away.

While I was clearly no match for Fiona, perhaps I had the edge on the pilot in EBZ. He had, by now, climbed out and was sitting cross-legged on the grass with his instructor, deep in conversation. A tow car sped along the perimeter track to meet them.

My last flight of the day started at exactly 4.45 and was over in some ten minutes. Later, with the words '*I have control*' ringing in my ears, I ran Fiona's wing and watched in envy as she lined up for a faultless aerotow.

Why is it that gliding is a man's sport and yet women often seem so much better at it? Time and again, just as I was getting the hang of things, a woman would put me firmly in my place. First it was Fiona and later, at Lasham, it was Hilary wheeling about the sky doing aerobatics. Only then, while talking to an instructor, did the reason become clear. 'Men think they know it all. They're often too over-confident. After all, they're brought up to know about boy's toys. Women are more willing to accept advice early on. They don't pretend to know everything. They're also very often more gentle with the controls and once they've learnt they tend to be fiercely competitive. The good ones are invariably very good.'

Two K13s waiting their turn in front of the single-seater version in which most people go solo. All three were made in West Germany, the spiritual home of gliding. The small hole in the nose of glider 113 is the pitot tube, through which air is forced to make the airspeed indicator work.

The weather had taken a turn for the worse by the time we packed up for the day. A greyish gloom obscured the July evening sky, and it didn't look promising. As I drove home that evening I felt the beginnings of an addiction growing. The precise details of every flight ran like a piano roll constantly through my mind. Flying time to date: one hour and four minutes. It seemed much longer. As the Honda banked into each turn my feet felt the resistance of phantom rudder pedals. The speedometer hovered around 55, the tachometer became the altimeter, the motorway the runway, the car in front the tug . . .

DAY THREE

G lider pilots hold the lives of tug pilots in their hands during an aerotow take-off. 'If you climb too steeply too soon there's a danger that you'll flip the tug forward into a dive,' explained Dave. 'That close to the ground there may not be time for the tug pilot to recover or release the tow. If that puts the fear of God into you, it needn't – tug crashes are very rare. But it's as well to know what could happen.'

Tugs work hard for their living. Engines designed to lift the aircraft alone have the additional burden of the glider and are stressed to the limit. Overheating, or over-rapid cooling as the hot engine descends, can fracture blocks or crack manifolds. The tug pilot has to manage his engine with skill, throttling back slowly and losing height gradually to allow the engine to reach normal operating temperature after a strenuous climb.

Although he has problems enough of his own the glider pilot should be aware of this. During the first few seconds of the take-off the glider's controls are sluggish and need to be moved fairly vigorously, but they rapidly become more sensitive as the tug reaches take-off speed. Initially the rudder and stick are worked independently to keep the glider in line and prevent either wing dropping; but very soon, as the wings gain lift, rudder and stick come together.

The wind had been increasing all morning. I had arrived late at the airfield, and the mist that hung over the land had evaporated to reveal another lowering

Glider pilots hold the lives of tug pilots in their hands. This young pilot, one of many at Booker who volunteer to tow gliders, gain valuable air time doing what is basically a thankless task. The line hanging down in front of him is the tow release, which allows him to detach the glider from his end if things get badly out of shape.

day. A dull greyness surrounded Booker and a dampness in the air foretold rain.

Again, in the small hours, the dreams had been of flying. Unavoidable hills sprang up in front of the gilder as it came in to land, and try as I might there seemed no way of averting disaster. There was no crash – just the softness of a pillow as I woke.

I waited in vain for a flight and at lunch-time wandered over to the hangars, where a Mosquito fighter-bomber, one of a number of old planes kept at Booker by a Second World War preservation society, was being readied for a flight to Canada. Beside her was a Spitfire. This was no fantasy, for 20 minutes later the Merlin engine was firing and the marvellous plane was bounding down the runway. To this day I cannot believe it was true.

———

My name was finally called soon after three o'clock. Once in the cockpit of EBZ we ran through the checks: CB SIFT CB. First 'C' for Controls. Shoulder straps loose, I peered over my shoulder, checking to see if the rudder obeyed my feet. Next the ailerons, port up, starboard down, then the other way before checking for full and free movement in all surfaces by waggling the stick in a circle with full left, and then right rudder. Then 'B' for Ballast.

Gliders are built to balance around an invisible

point somewhere in the middle of the fuselage, just about one third of the way back along the wing from the leading edge. A heavier than average pilot in the front seat will bring the centre of gravity (Cg) forward tending, to cause the glider to take a nose-down trim and consequently fly faster. Too much weight in the back has the opposite effect.

Each glider nevertheless balances differently. A placard in the cockpit indicates the acceptable weight limits and this varies with every glider. If the pilot in the front is too light, lead ballast is bolted under the front seat to bring the Cg forward. If the Cg is too far back it can upset the stability and make it more likely for any stall to develop into a flat spin, from which there is often no recovery.

Too much weight too far forward can overload the wings during manoeuvres and make it harder for the pilot to trim or to bring the nose up to achieve the correct flying speed. With both Dave and I weighing in at under 12 stone we were well within the limits. 'OK ballast,' I called.

'S' is for Straps, tight and locked. 'Locked and secure,' came the reply from behind me. 'I' is for Instruments: the altimeter, airspeed indicator and variometer all read zero. The K 13 has no flaps, so 'F' was passed over. 'T' is for Trim, that little lever on the right which allows the pilot to adjust the glider's attitude in flight; forward a touch for take-off to counteract any tendency for the glider to climb too rapidly. 'C' is for Canopy, locked and secure. 'B' is for Brakes: back on the lever, check they are operating and then forward to see if they close together and further still to lock them shut until needed.

Fiona materialised with the tow rope. 'Open,' I called through the sliding window to my left, pulling

Zeroing the altimeter, one of the CB SIFT CB checks prior to flight. Instrumentation is very basic in a training glider like the K 13, but can become extremely sophisticated in high-performance gliders. Pilot skill and judgement are still the most important factors.

the yellow toggle. The ring was placed in the release hook. 'Close.' Fiona pulled hard to check it was secure as I called out, 'Are we all clear above and behind?' and circled a finger in the air.

They'll tell you a story of the novice pilot, strapped into his seat, calling out, 'Are we all clear above and below?' to which the instructor drily replied, 'We're not learning to fly a submarine.' Whatever the truth of the story it's certainly true that the visual check is important. The pilot is blind to what's going on behind the glider. Another glider may be landing. A winch line may have fallen across the runway. Like every routine it must not become routine. At Lasham they also insist that the pilot calls out the checks rather than run the risk of misinterpretation. A vague 'OK, then?' is misleading.

Next I gave the one-finger signal for take-up slack and the tug rolled forward slowly until the line came taut. 'All out,' two fingers. The pitch of the engine increased, hurling little tufts of grass over the canopy. The glider swayed forward, lurching to the right. I jabbed the left rudder to straighten us. The left wing began to drop. I swung the stick to the right and the right wing dropped.

With the stick fully back we began to skate over the grass, lunging wildly from side to side like a struggling salmon on a line. The nose reared up to meet the oncoming blast. 'Christ, the tug,' I thought, jamming the stick forward again. The glider dropped 20 feet towards the ground, bounced once and, as I dragged the stick back again, shot up into the air.

'OK, I have control,' said the familiar voice from the back. 'In this headwind the glider wants to fly early. Don't be afraid to let her lift as soon as she's ready, but keep her below 15 feet until the tug's off the ground. It's better to get off early than keep her on the ground: it reduces the drag caused by the wheel and lets the tug pick up speed quickly for his own take-off.

'I know you're worried about lifting the tug's tail,' Dave continued, 'but as long as you keep to about 15 feet that's fine. If you hold her down there's a danger that you'll climb too steeply too soon as the speed rises. The elevator is very sensitive at tugging speeds and there's a danger you'll get into what's called Pilot Induced Oscillation.'

The buffeting had increased as we swept over the boundary, banking slowly to the right and climbing at a steady three knots. Volleys of turbulence jerked the wings. I felt the stick make the urgent little movements, keeping the wings in line with the tug's. 'OK, you have control,' said Dave. 'But relax. Don't grip

The stages of a smooth aerotow, demonstrated here by Dave Byass. Controls are sluggish at first. The glider lifts off earlier than the tug, within 100 yards if there is a strong headwind, and is kept at head height until the tug is airborne . . .

. . . the wings follow the tug's as it starts a gentle turn to the right over the perimeter track at just under 100 feet . . .

. . . before continuing its turn over the M40 motorway, just visible at the right of the picture.

At 500 feet, airspeed just over 60 knots, Dave follows the tug towards the horizon in the correct position. Above him the yaw string flies straight and true. All he has to do now is gently match the tug's movements as the combination climbs towards the pull-off altitude. Note the emergency canopy release knob in the foreground.

the stick so hard. Try to anticipate and don't overcorrect or you'll start flying erratically.'

The tug continued its turn and I followed it round trying to keep stick and rudder movements in 'sync'. The tug remained just above my horizon. The tow-rope arced gently downwards and up to meet the tail.

During an aerotow the tug pilot is in command. If at any stage things get out of hand he will waggle his wings, the signal for the glider pilot to release immediately. Any delay and the tug pilot will release from his own end. If he thinks you have a problem your end – the air-brakes may be out, for example – he will waggle his rudder.

In the unlikely event of the glider pilot not being able to release his end he should fly out to the left of the tow and waggle his wings. The tug pilot will then head back and release the glider his end at (hopefully) the correct height and position for a normal landing. The tow-rope may well release from the glider if the toggle is kept pulled and fall away as the glider comes into land. If things really get out of hand the tow-rope is designed to break at about 100 pounds pressure.

We released at 1,600 feet. Two sharp pulls on the toggle (the second one to make sure the hook has released), the rope spun away and we banked gently, nose up to gain a little altitude before settling into level flight. 'Trim for about 45 knots,' said Dave. The stick became lighter as I pulled the lever half an inch or so back. 'Now we'll try some stalling,' he said. 'I have control.'

Stalling takes place when the wings lose their ability

Aerotowing

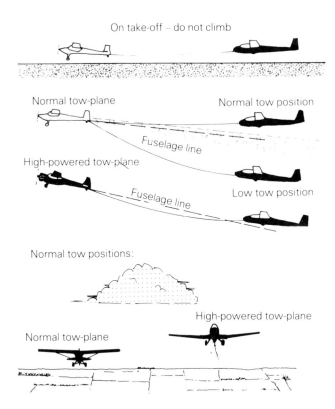

On take-off – do not climb

Normal tow-plane

Normal tow position

Fuselage line

High-powered tow-plane

Fuselage line

Low tow position

Normal tow positions:

High-powered tow-plane

Normal tow-plane

The various stages of aerotow from take-off to level flight. The correct attitude is maintained in relation to the tug's position above the horizon.

to support the weight of glider and its crew. It's caused by a combination of low speed and/or too high an angle of attack – that is, the wings meeting the airflow at too steep an angle, thereby causing the air to 'break away' from the upper surfaces.

The easiest way to induce a stall is to fly nose-up until the speed drops to the point at which the controls become sluggish. The glider begins to shake as the air detaches itself from the upper surface of the wings and begins to fall away. Usually one wing will stall before another. The instinctive reaction is to try and counter-act the drop by an opposite movement of the stick, but this only exaggerates the stall. The wing drops further and you find yourself in what's called an 'incipient spin'.

The correct action is simple. Stick gently forward to reduce the angle of attack and opposite rudder to stop the swing of the nose. As the glider picks up speed the

Stalling occurs when the wing meets the airflow at too high an angle of attack. The air detaches from the top side and the wing loses lift, no longer able to support the weight of the glider.

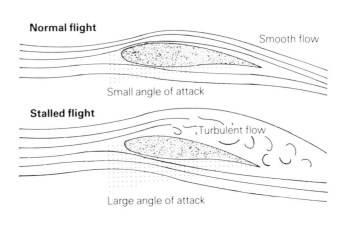

Normal flight

Smooth flow

Small angle of attack

Stalled flight

Turbulent flow

Large angle of attack

One wing will usually stall, and drop, before the other and what is called an incipient spin will begin. Stick forward a little and opposite rudder will correct the stall which is usually, but not always, associated with flying too slowly.

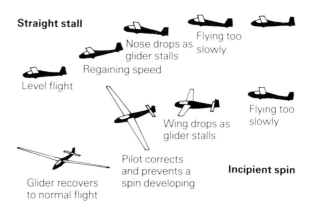

Straight stall

Flying too slowly

Nose drops as glider stalls

Regaining speed

Level flight

Flying too slowly

Wing drops as glider stalls

Pilot corrects and prevents a spin developing

Incipient spin

Glider recovers to normal flight

wings regain their lift and the glider swoops down out of the stall, and the incipient spin is ironed out before it becomes a full spin.

Our K 13 liked to stall at about 30 knots. 'First let's check there's nothing below us,' said the voice from the back. Dave banked steeply to the right in a full 360° turn, peering down below the wing root. Levelling off, he then eased the stick back slowly until the wind noise dropped away to nothing and the airframe began to shudder – the sign that the airflow over the wings was detaching. The altimeter started to drop rapidly as we sank towards the field, nose slightly above the horizon, airspeed indicator hovering around 28, left wing slightly down.

'Now recover!'

I grabbed the stick and pushed it forward and then corrected the incipient spin with a touch of opposite rudder. The shuddering stopped, the nose dropped sharply and I found myself looking almost vertically down towards a red-brick farmhouse. The speed rose to 70 knots. The wind noise increased to a roar as the nose swept upwards. It felt as if I had suddenly put on 20 pounds. The glider bounded towards the horizon like a car breasting a humpback bridge. 'Overdid the stick a touch,' said the voice. I felt a little bit sick.

With the stick gently back again the nose levelled off and speed returned to 45 knots. The wind noise

At about 1,000 feet the glider banks to the right and, with air-brakes slightly out, drops to the level of the photographer's aircraft. The left-hand aileron can clearly be seen, raising that wing by increasing the lift. The right aileron is correspondingly up. The elevator is set for level flight, the rudder slightly turned to compensate for 'aileron drag' in the turn.

decreased. Once you learn never to counteract a wing drop by using opposite stick, stall recovery is one of the more natural processes in the learning curve. By now the airfield was in sight, 700 feet below and to our right. *'I have control.'* The wind, which had been blowing at, perhaps, 15 knots at ground level, had increased with height, an effect that's called 'wind gradient'. The friction of the ground slows the air immediately above it. The higher you go the stronger the wind as the ground effect lessens, so at 700 feet we were probably being swept downwind at more like 25 knots. Add that to our airspeed and the ground was disappearing behind our right wing at a rate of 70 knots.

At 500 feet it was time to turn in towards the boundary, losing height as we banked 45° to our right to avoid being swept past the point at which it would be impossible to make the field. We trimmed to 60 knots, a little faster than normal to combat the headwind, and Dave eased out half air-brakes, increasing our stalling speed, breaking up the wings' lift. EBZ seemed to hover for a few seconds over the motionless field and then, at 15 feet, the nose levelled and we alighted like an ungainly duck, slightly tail-first in a copybook landing.

It takes a brave man to instruct glider pilots, I thought, as we ran through the flight, still strapped into our seats. 'It's more stressful than you think,' claimed Dave. 'Especially taking off. My main worry is landing after an aborted take-off, say if the cable

Speed and height can always be converted to the pilot's advantage, so never fly 'low and slow'. During the final stages of landing there is a risk of stalling in the final turn and there may be too little height to allow the glider to convert whatever height is left into speed.

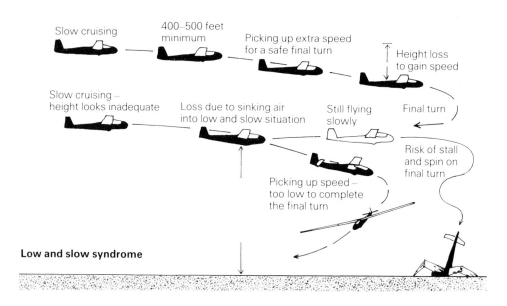

Slow cruising

400–500 feet minimum

Picking up extra speed for a safe final turn

Height loss to gain speed

Slow cruising – height looks inadequate

Loss due to sinking air into low and slow situation

Still flying slowly

Final turn

Risk of stall and spin on final turn

Picking up speed – too low to complete the final turn

Low and slow syndrome

breaks or the tug pilot has to wave us off for any reason. If we're low enough it's possible to land straight ahead, no problem, but there's a transition period. Are we high enough to make a safe turn and land back near the launch point – or should we be looking for a suitable field ahead?

'Once we're up the guy in front doesn't realise how much is going on that he doesn't know about. He's only aware of keeping his controls smooth. He probably hasn't a clue about where we are in relation to the field.'

The last approach and landing in strong winds had impressed on me the importance of being aware of height and location. Any delay on the final turn can leave you too far downwind to claw back into the wind for the landing. In strong winds it is better to turn earlier.

'*Never get low and slow.*' The words ran through my brain like a mantra. I began to realise the logic of those turns, aware that the instructor is not only telling you what to do but mentally looking ahead to the eventual landing.

———

Flight seven was destined to be my last at Booker. By now low rain-clouds were spitting on us. The wind had also increased, blowing at an angle to the runway, trying to 'weathercock' the tail. During the first few seconds of take-off the rudder is turned away from the crosswind to counteract the drift. Once airborne both glider and tug are flying in this moving block of air and the effect of crosswind plays little part in control. Only the ground slips away.

At 1,600 feet we found a two-knot lift which neatly cancelled out the K 13's natural tendency to sink at about the same rate. Circling in the rising air, inside wing-tip feeling for the centre of lift, we managed to prolong our flight enough to give another few precious minutes to get my feet and hands working in harmony. Too soon, it seemed, a glance revealed the airfield far out under the horizon.

As the wind bore us away the ground slipped like a carpet from beneath our wings. A few minutes later lift had turned to sink – rapid sink, sucking us downwards. We turned for home, the eery wailing sound of the variometer filling the cockpit.

At 500 feet we banked steeply towards the airfield and I had control. Too far. The nose was pointing downwards towards a line of light aircraft to the right of the main tarmac runway. Back to the left. '*Watch your speed!*' came the urgent voice from behind my

At the height of a double-decker bus the glider is rounded out, ie the nose is levelled and the glider allowed to alight in its own time rather than being flown down. At 5 feet, with the air-brakes open, the glider will land itself before very long.

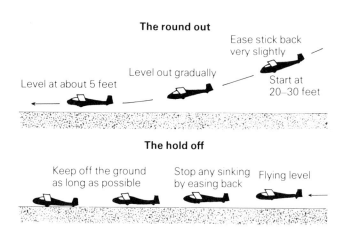

The round out

Ease stick back very slightly

Level out gradually

Level at about 5 feet

Start at 20–30 feet

The hold off

Keep off the ground as long as possible

Stop any sinking by easing back

Flying level

head. 'Keep on checking it every couple of seconds.'

I hardly needed to look at the dial. The wind noise was enough to warn me that we were heading for the ground at 70 knots. I trimmed back to 55, banking a fraction to the left ... more turbulence as the glider fell through the wind gradient ... nose pointing slightly into the crosswind, the glider rounded out at the height of a double-decker bus. I steered the fuselage into line as the ground swam up to enclose us.

'Don't let the nose drop. Keep her off as long as possible,' said Dave. The left wing dropped a little as skid met grass. Everything was happening too fast. I jabbed the rudder to bring the nose to the left and the glider skated round in a tight arc towards the control bus. The left wing was on the ground, dragging us round. Figures sprang towards us. The bus disappeared over my right shoulder as the glider headed towards an expensive-looking single-seater waiting in line ...

Drained of its energy, EBZ slowed and stopped. There had been so much to think about, so much to take in. Too much. I had lost co-ordination. Having felt elated after the previous flight I now battled with dejection. I wanted to get straight back in and show that I could fly, prove I wasn't an idiot. I was angry at spoiling an otherwise perfect flight.

The wind now swept the airfields with brutal little gusts. A cold front was upon us and there would be no more flying that day. Back in the lecture-room, the rain drummed on the wooden roof as Dave ran through the landing procedure on the blackboard to his small, weather-bound audience – a lecture he must have delivered many times before.

'There are two stages in landing,' he told us. 'The approach, which is largely a matter of judgment, and the landing, which relies on correct handling. Select your approach speed. On a K 13 that's about 50 knots plus five knots for every 10 knots of wind-speed. Some gliders are slower.

'We fly faster on the approach for two reasons. First, to leave a margin for error in case we need to turn in quickly; second, to keep a reserve of energy to avoid the "low and slow syndrome".' So *that's* why we fly fast, I thought to myself, just when it seems we should be trying to go as slowly as possible.

'If you stall twenty feet from the ground because you're flying too slowly,' continued Dave, 'you'll have no time to drop the nose, pick up speed and round out. K 13s weigh about half a ton. You'll probably be OK, but the glider won't like it very much. Always remember the wind gradient: air near the ground is slowed by the friction of passing over the surface and is more turbulent.

'As you approach the landing-point about 50 feet up look towards the other end of the field. If you only look 100 yards ahead you'll hit the ground hard. At 20 feet level off parallel to the ground. The normal attitude on the round out slows the glider, avoiding stress on the airframe as it touches down. There may be rabbit holes. If you hit a bump at 45 knots you're still at flying speed.' Dave aimed a knowing smile at Pete, whom I'd seen bounding down the strip at exactly that speed two hours earlier.

'You must hold off landing for as long as you can – then, as the glider touches, gradually move the stick right back to avoid hammering the nose skid. Remember that you're still flying until the glider stops. And whatever you do don't move the stick forward very near the ground. A small movement is acceptable if you find you've rounded out much too early, but not too much or you'll drive the glider unto the ground before you have time to move the stick back to stop it sinking.'

A nervous laugh did the rounds as Dave began to explain the effect of air-brakes. 'The air-brakes control the rate of descent. That's their primary function, rather than to slow you. On a K 13 air-brakes reduce the rate of descent from about 25:1, which is normal, to about 8:1. Air-brakes also increase the speed at which you stall, which is another reason for keeping speed up on the approach. Don't open them very near the ground, and be wary of using them at low level. Approach with about half-brake; the longer you hold off the better the landing.' The

quicker you get down the better, I thought – no point in prolonging the agony.

'You must have chosen your landing-point by the time you make your base leg. Choose your aiming point before the final turn. It can be large but select a point about 30 yards into the field. The point simply enables you to relate your landing to the space available – a reference point. This should stay stationary on the final approach as you control the rate of descent with the air-brakes. Always monitor speed, controlling it gently with the elevator.

'Let's take an extreme. If you point the nose at the aiming point at, say, eighty knots and round out fifty feet above it, it'll be too late to control descent with the brakes.'

'Sounds a little dangerous,' I offered.

'That depends,' replied Dave. 'I've known people just freeze. Others get what I call "landing lever syndrome". They go into brain failure on approach, jam the brakes out and expect automatically to land. That's a sure recipe for undershooting. Every time anyone undershoots and lands on the boundary you can be certain they've had their air-brakes open too early. Keep the aiming point stationary by judicious use of the brakes. If the aiming point starts disappear-

TOP LEFT: EBZ approaches the landing area for a perfect touchdown. Coming in low over the perimeter fence with air-brakes part open, the pilot will be trimmed to 55 knots to overcome the higher stalling speed.

LEFT: At about the height of a bus the pilot rounds out by easing back gently on the stick and the glider settles onto the field slightly tail down in the perfect attitude.

ABOVE: The glider touches down and then drops forward onto the wheel and nose skid.

ing beneath you – that is, you're overshooting – use more brake, and vice versa.

'Remember also to allow more height over trees. Small obstructions cause significant "sink" and if you haven't got height or speed you're in trouble.'

Dave's talk gave us no more than an insight into what was coming next – if the weather picked up. Until that point I'd not even touched the air-brakes, for example.

What little circuit planning I'd been aware of so far had more to do with Dave's careful eye on the general direction of my meanderings over the Buckinghamshire countryside. Circuit planning is all about judgment, constantly relating your approach to the field, turning with sufficient height and speed to be able to pick an aiming point and land as close beyond it as your round out will allow.

Rope breaks call for quick decisions. 'The size of a field is more important than the surface,' said Dave, 'though grass is better than crop. You learn to distinguish what's in the fields by experience. Usually the darker the field the higher the crop. They can do a lot of damage to a glider, though grass fields can be full of holes. As you climb after take-off think about where you could land if the rope breaks. Always be prepared.'

———

Thus far we had only skimmed the surface of knowledge, but the briefing had hinted at things to come. To date I had one hour and 29 minutes flying time in my green log-book, had taken control briefly on the aerotow, practised interminable turning, recovered from a few gentle stalls and had a hand in that last landing. There was so much more to learn: in fact at the end of the day the list seemed if anything to grow longer – practising for cable breaks, for example, is a vital part of the training of new glider pilots. At some stage our instructor would pull the release toggle prematurely. What would we do? As if control, take-off and landing hadn't been enough already to think about during those last three days we had spent at Booker . . .

Frustration seemed an inevitable part of the learning process, but at least I knew now that I had the makings of a pilot and the mistakes I'd made had also been made by countless novice pilots before me. To discover that I was no worse than average was comforting – and exactly matched my own gut feeling.

Nevertheless, the dream of solo flight seemed as

impossibly distant as ever as I climbed on to the dripping seat of the bike and headed despondently for home. To make further progress gliding would have to become a part of life, not a just a weekend activity. 'Never refuse the chance of a flight, no matter what the weather looks like.'

This particular batch of English summer weather looked set to dampen all but the most ardent enthusiast. Glistening wet gliders sat dejectedly under grey skies, and the forecast held little encouragement. For two days I waited for a break, waking early to listen to the radio for any sign of an improvement. But none came.

Slowly I slipped back into City life. Booker receded and, with it, the dream of flying. Countless times in the following months I determined to resume where I had left off – but something always cropped up to make my excuses seem plausible. Flying was not a way of life, yet. The taste was in my mouth but there was nothing to chew on. The notebook in which I'd kept a record of those flights was tucked away in a drawer with the log-book. Out of sight and, almost, out of mind. And there it stayed for the best part of two years . . .

DAY FOUR

A year and ten months passed before my feet again felt the controls of a glider. I cannot count the day I spent at the Auckland Gliding Club in New Zealand, a little grass strip tucked away among the hills south of the city. I was then an enchanted passenger, no more, floating over a countryside as green and lush as Devon. Ahead, glistening in the distance, Auckland basked among the islands of the Hauraki Gulf. To the east lay the Coromandel Peninsula, below us the Drury Hills. My log-book was back in England. There's no record of those two trips and I prefer to regard them as flights of fantasy.

While they were nevertheless vital in keeping the embers of enthusiasm glowing, a greater spur to my ambition of becoming a glider pilot was perhaps an old friend of mine called Jason. I discovered in him an eager listener as I recounted my brief encounters with the air at Booker, but I never expected my words to take root so quickly.

Jason announced a short time later that he had booked a three-week holiday in Australia. What he never admitted, until he arrived back in England, was that one of those weeks had been spent gliding. In the clear blue skies above the Murray River at Tucumwal in New South Wales, Jason had gone solo in 23 flights. In just over a week he had spent over 11 hours aloft – and he couldn't wait to tell me.

My tally was pitiful in comparison. Whenever the chance arose, I admit to having announced, when the conversation was suitably hushed, 'Oh yes, I go gliding,' but never in the presence of a real pilot.

My log-book spoke briefly of seven flights, a total of 89 minutes in the air. It was something to impress most people. No matter that I was no more than a millimetre along the flight-path to solo. I couldn't honestly say that I'd even controlled an entire flight from aerotow to landing.

But inside there now stirred an embryonic pilot. Despite the frustrations, the waiting and the weather I promised to return. A summer passed. The slightest glimpse of that graceful T-shape hanging in the clouds caused a lump in the throat and a quickening of the pulse.

One June afternoon, as I was steering a narrow-boat down the Thames, I looked up to see the silhouette of a glider against the sun. From being perfectly content chugging along between the tall grass I suddenly felt earthbound, restricted to the confines of the bank. High above me the pilot of that slender form would be looking down on the glistening silver snail's track of the river, and our dark blob crawling imperceptibly towards Henley.

————

If you're lucky enough to live within easy reach of a gliding club a nominal sum will buy an introductory flight. Technically speaking they are called Air Experience flights, a cross between a test drive and a joy-ride. Every evening at around six a busload of punters, the typing pool from a nearby office or a couple of teenagers on a 'dare', will draw up in the club car park, sign their names to a form, hand over between £10 and £30 and wait their turn apprehensively.

Half an hour or so later they'll come bowling into land, grinning ear to ear. Sometimes you'll see an elderly gentleman with a military bearing buckle himself into the front seat to relive a postwar memory. Perhaps he was one of the hundreds who, whilst stationed in Germany after the war, had signed up for five shillings a week to learn gliding in the capable hands of a recently demobbed ex-Luftwaffe pilot.

Most clubs, nearly 100 in Britain, are happy to introduce you to gliding on a casual basis, and it's a far easier process than booking a test drive in the latest BMW. While casual flying is an expensive way to gain experience and lacks the continuity that brings fast results, for many people it's the only way they can find the time to fly. Some people simply cannot afford the cost of a five-day course which can range from £150 to nearly £300 including board and lodging at the club.

Lasham Gliding Society's headquarters occupy a former wartime Spitfire and Mosquito airfield in the heart of the Hampshire countryside near Alton. K 13s and a variety of Lasham's 200 gliders are parked ready to be towed out and up into what looks like a good summer's sky for thermals.

The cost of learning to glide compares well with any adventure sport and cannot be equated with learning to fly a powered aircraft, which is expensive. The only commodity that does get used up in prodigious quantities is time. Without a share in your own glider you're at the mercy of the availability of club gliders, but there are hundreds of pilots who would not dream of buying their own, preferring to join a club and fly on a casual basis, paying for each flight at the current rate – about £15 an hour, including the winch launch.

Most people learn to glide during a series of week-long courses. Using only the average holiday entitlement a pilot could expect to go solo well within a year, and often sooner if he or she is keen enough. A gliding course is, in itself, an ideal holiday. There are few places more removed from the bustle of everyday life than an airfield, and in fine weather there's nothing quite like messing around among gliders with a couple of good books, a thermos of orange juice and tube of sun screen.

In five days a minimum number of flights is guaranteed, usually about ten aerotows or 24 winch launches. If bad weather stops flying, and that's rare even in Britain, the lost flights are credited for another day. The course fee will usually include membership for three months, during which time you receive a discount on further courses.

On a brilliant morning in May I found myself once more bowling along the English country lanes in search of an elusive airfield that I could sense but could not yet see. Though signs to Lasham village did appear, someone had cunningly devised a way to hide 30 acres of flat grass among a screen of rolling valleys and woodland. Eventually, I turned into the car park of the Lasham Gliding Society.

Lasham occupies a wartime airfield 600 feet up on a plateau north-east of Alton in Hampshire, surrounded by lush countryside in the heart of one of the most affluent counties in Britain. Like so many the airfield was built by the RAF (in 1942) and was once the home of Spitfire and Mosquito squadrons – as a plaque in the clubhouse, set up by the World War Aircraft Preservation Society, proudly attests.

A 2,000-foot tarmac runway faces west into the prevailing winds, bisected by two shorter runways. The western end is occupied by Dan Air with a servicing facility for its commercial fleet. A mile or so to the east, tucked away opposite the end of the main runway beside some huts, a sorry collection of old aircraft belonging to the World War Aircraft Preservation Society awaits restoration – a Hunter, a Vampire, a couple of helicopters and an ex-Luftwaffe Starfighter. Old aero-engines litter the ground.

Lasham is the largest gliding society in Europe with unrivalled facilities, and over 20 clubs and 145 gliders are based there. Flying is year-round. Until recently the Chief Flying Instructor was Derek Piggott, undoubtedly the most celebrated glider pilot in postwar years; a year earlier and I would probably have been taking lessons from him. Having come here with the avowed intention of writing a book, I was in some ways glad that the author of the most comprehensive collection of gliding books was no longer in charge.

Piggott's job is now held by Terry Joint, assisted by Malcolm Hook, while the society is managed by 'Phil' Phillips. It's not long before you recognise that a friendly rivalry exists between Booker and Lasham, with both having nurtured some of the best pilots in the world. Over 60% of Lasham's 750 members are, in Terry Joint's opinion, 'very good' and 50% own their gliders or a share in one.

Breakfast was being served when I arrived carrying a holdall and a brand new Italian Air Force flying suit with more pockets than the Artful Dodger's overcoat. I bought a mug of coffee and killed time trying to detect some common characteristics among the dozen or so glider pilots seated around the canteen, but just when I thought I'd cracked it someone would turn up

Terry Joint, Lasham's highly qualified Chief Flying Instructor, looking suitably aeronautical at the controls of a K 13.

who refused to conform to my stereotype. A lanky middle-aged man in tracksuit and trainers wandered in and started chatting with a group near the window overlooking the perimeter track. Clearly a novice, I thought. No co-ordination. I saw him again that evening carrying the barograph that attested to his five-hour soaring flight, 50 kilometres cross-country.

At nine sharp the office opened and I scrawled my name on a couple of forms, studiously ignoring the small print. Again, as at Booker, there were four of us sharing a glider and instructor. 'Sorry, couldn't provide any female company this time,' said a voice behind me, which I later found belonged to the Chief Flying Instructor. 'Usually we have a pretty even mix. You're just unlucky.'

Terry Joint knocked the ash from his cigarette and, after introducing himself formally, led the four of us into a lecture-room where a dozen or so other people were drawn up around a small video screen. Most of the group looked much like me, dressed casually in jeans and T-shirt, but there were others with the look I recognised from Booker.

Terry is a cheerful, relaxed sort of man with the tanned face and twinkling eyes of a pilot used to spending long hours in a cockpit searching for thermals. A modest but awesomely accomplished pilot, he holds all the highest awards and has flown in many major gliding competitions.

Three courses were operating that week – a basic course, advanced course and an aerobatic course. There were eight of us on the basic course, four to a glider with an instructor each. The advanced course ('You'll recognise them, they're the ones in the smart planes') and the aerobatic courses were already on the field.

'Don't feel you're the underdogs,' said Terry before switching on a slide show introducing us to Lasham. 'You're just as important to us as the others here this week and if you have anything you want to ask, any complaints about the food, your instructor, anything – don't leave it until the end of the week, just ask.'

Among other valuable tips the film advised us to be careful not to confuse our airfield with nearby Odiham, an RAF helicopter base. I remembered my efforts to locate Booker all those months ago and took special heed. 'You can't mistake us as we've got our own golf ball,' explained Terry, referring to the satellite tracking dish which we could just make out from where we sat. 'Unfortunately Odiham has one too, but theirs is much smaller.'

Basic safety instructions, grounded in common sense, included not walking diagonally towards the

Gerrard Dale's love of flying brought him as an instructor to Lasham, where he lives with his wife in a mobile home on the perimeter track. At weekends he flies his own glider; you can't get much more keen or dedicated than that.

launch point, avoiding winch cables and reminding us that airfields are dangerous places to walk about with your head buried in the ground. 'Airfields are good places to make mistakes.' And I was to make most of them during the next five days.

The air of studied informality that I'd enjoyed at Booker was again evident, but here too it was veined with a relaxed professionalism that at once put us at ease without coming over as being too casual. Gliding, after all, is a serious sport.

If Booker had rooted the sapling of addiction, Lasham saw it sprout green leaves and begin to support its own weight. Once again there was only a limited delay in getting us into the cockpit and up into the inviting, clear skies. Like someone who last rode a bike in his childhood the first flight, my eighth following the seven at Booker, brought all the old sensations flooding back. This time the voice in the back belonged to Gerrard Dale, or 'G' for short, a talented musician and teacher turned glider pilot who cheerfully admitted to being 'an airfield bum'.

But he sells himself short with that description. In his early thirties, living with his wife in a small mobile home by the perimeter track, with his own glider nearby, G was living proof of the phrase that I had heard time and time again: 'Gliding is a way of life.' G had begged and borrowed the money for his first glider and by judicious trading up was now the owner of a 12-year-old Jantar, which he flew for pleasure at the weekends.

Lasham has over 90 qualified instructors but only two, Terry Joint and Malcolm Hook, are full-time professionals. During the summer the society takes on four or five additional instructors, one of whom is G.

It's not good enough for an instructor simply to be a good pilot; he must also be a good teacher. And a teacher without formal training needs either to be an eccentric, able to inspire by sheer force of character, or a natural inspirer. G, who could hardly be called an eccentric – like Nigel Palmer, who was to take the other four on our course – was both a gifted pilot and exceptional instructor. Not once during the week did that quiet voice raise in tone above an authoritative urgency, despite my attempts to fly our K 13 into the ground on more than one occasion.

'What have you done then?' asked G, and I told him as honestly as I could about the aborted course at Booker all those months ago. I tried to sound as if I knew at least something about gliding, without coming over as an expert. There was little point in pretending that I knew anything other than the very basics. After all, I hadn't even landed the thing totally hands-on yet. I handed him my old log-book and let him read the bare facts for himself.

Continuity in instructors is important, and inevitably there were lessons to relearn after such a lapse of time. The evidence in my log-book told only a small part of the story, and that first flight at Lasham gave both of us a chance to assess each other.

No matter how competent you may appear on the ground the bullshit stops when the nose-wheel lifts off the tarmac. As G handed over the controls to me I could imagine him watching the movements on the stick and rudder. I knew I was no 'natural', but I was determined not to come over as 'below average'.

G told me later that he had never flown with a natural pilot. Some of the older instructors had come across a couple in a long career, but most are boringly predictable, making the same mistakes at the same time. Ironically perhaps, the handful of exceptional pilots are terrifying to teach; never making mistakes, they seldom find themselves in dangerous situations and therefore the instructor has to engineer problems before they occur naturally.

Learning invariably comes through making errors. The pilot who makes none must not only be forced into error but slapped down every time he gets too over-enthusiastic or confident. 'Ninety-eight per cent are average and two per cent exceptional – and it doesn't take long to spot them,' said Terry. 'They're dangerous and good, although they don't all have blond hair and good looks!'

I was clearly not one of these. Having always learned slowly from my mistakes I was encouraged whenever G told me that what I had or had not just done was 'quite normal' at that particular phase and 'would soon feel natural with a few more flights'. In particular rudder control was causing problems. A glider like the K 13, which has a large rudder, needs only a little nudge to counteract the tendency of the nose to swing away from the lower wing – aileron drag – in a turn.

I found it helped to recite the sequence out aloud for those first flights. For a left turn, for example, it went like this: 'Look out over shoulder to the right, through the nose to the left and back ahead. Stick and rudder together. Stick back, rudder back. Lookout around the horizon, keep the angle of bank steady, watch the yaw string to keep the fuselage heading into the airflow using a little rudder,' and so on.

As the tow rope bounded forward G pointed down to our right to a little ploughed field in a hollow. 'That's the kind of place you'd find a thermal. When you're looking for lift, imagine what it would be like on the ground. Just think how hot it would be sitting in that hollow – a real sun-trap.'

Sure enough, as the wing swept over the brown stain a bubble of air took us, sending the vario into an ecstatic leap toward $+4$; keeping her circling over the spot, we were being pushed upwards at four knots. Free height – height that owed nothing to the pulse of an internal combustion engine. Gliders run on empty.

In its simplest form, 'thermals are like bubbles of hot water rising in a bath. When they meet air cold enough to cause condensation, clouds form.' Around the edge of this thermal bubble the air is invariably sinking as cooler air is sucked in to take its place. You can feel this effect on a hot summer's day. There you are sunbathing, perhaps, when all of sudden a cold wind brushes across your chest, filling the partial vacuum left as another bubble detaches itself from the ground and mushrooms upwards.

The theory behind soaring flight is complex, relying a great deal on pilot intuition for practical application. During a five-day course it's touched on only briefly, but the effects can be felt at any time. Sitting in front of G, I could sense his elation every time the vario moved upwards. How galling it must be to be wasting a perfectly good soaring day teaching someone like me. Never once did he admit to that, but I knew he must have felt it.

———

The skies above Lasham remained blue. Too blue to be a perfect soaring day, but the gentle breeze and smooth air were ideal for learning. Flights took off and landed, and the daily ritual of the airfield went on. There were flights to log, gliders to retrieve and countless conversations to be interrupted in the constant business of keeping the gliders flying. The outside world never intruded.

Lasham's control bus was a step up from the BA bus used at Booker. Two banks of car headlights set up high over the front cab signalled to the winch driver, nearly a mile away down the runway, the vital instructions that controlled the launch. Long flashes invited him to '*Take up slack*', while urgent flashing signified '*All Out*'.

A portable radio communicated the same instructions to the tug pilot. Every five minutes a glider was either hurled into the sky by winch or towed over the

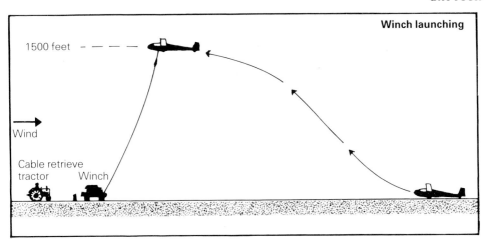

Winch launching

1500 feet

Wind

Cable retrieve
tractor   Winch

boundary hedge behind one of three tugs circling and landing. Before long everyone was taking their turn in the running of the landing-point, running the wing, manning the radio or winch signals or driving the Honda four-wheel buggy to retrieve gliders from distant corners of the airfield.

The tug pilot who took us up that morning was a young man, building up air-time before joining an

Launching by winch is cheap and effective, but height is limited to about 1,500 feet. It's the most common form of launching for small clubs and has reached a high level of development.

A launch controller relays the glider pilot's name from his log to the tug. Controlling the launch procedure is easier with a radio and saves going near the propeller.

63

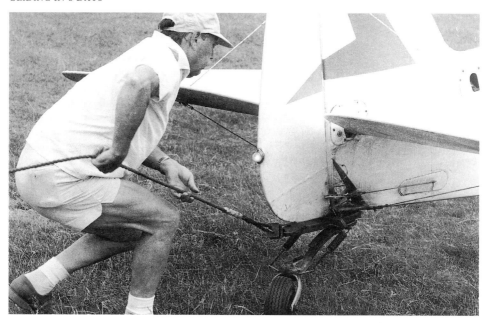

The tug end of the tow rope is attached to a special release hook that can be tripped by the pilot if things get completely out of hand. They very rarely do, but there are times when the tug pilot may need to release the glider in a hurry. The tug's fuselage may need to be strengthened before it is passed to tow gliders, though the actual loads are surprisingly low once the glider is airborne.

airline as a commercial pilot. Tugging provides excellent practice, with up to 50 take-offs and landings a day.

The tug that took us up was a French-built Rallye. 'She's really just a squadron of rivets flying in loose formation,' the pilot told me as he stepped down from the cockpit for a drink. It sounded like an old joke – and evidently was. Tugs are too valuable to treat badly: their life is hard enough without neglecting routine maintenance, and it's often expensive to insure a light aircraft for glider towing. The fuselage has to be specially strengthened or strong enough to take the sudden jerks on the rope, although the strain once in level flight is probably little more than 60 pounds or so.

The tow rope is attached to a release hook under the tail skid. A toggle in the cockpit releases the rope in an emergency, though no one I spoke to could last remember when that had occurred. Nevertheless, all tug pilots are aware of the tragedy that took place some years back when a reasonably experienced glider pilot got too high on tow and pitched the tug into the ground, killing the pilot.

My ninth flight, the second of the day, reinforced my turning. At 1,500 feet a flight of swifts provided clear evidence of thermals. As insects are drawn upwards by the rising air the birds follow them, enjoying a moving feast. Pilots in America tell of soaring flights in the company of eagles, surely the ultimate test in mutual tolerance.

There were no eagles above Lasham. Some of the flies that the swifts missed were plastered to the leading edge of our wings as we landed. 'Keeping the glider spotless becomes an obsession with competition pilots,' said G. The tiniest blemish on the smooth aerofoil can cause a noticeable loss of performance. Competition pilots take things to extremes. The American team at the 1989 world championship, in Austria, came in for a great deal of criticism over the use of a built-in debugging device on the leading edge.

Study the surface of a high-performance glider and you will find that every join between wing and fuselage, tail and rudder is carefully taped over to prevent air escaping from the high-pressure side below to the low-pressure side, that provides the lift, on the upper surface. Before a competition a glider pilot will polish his machine with infinite care. 'Remind me tomorrow morning to get you all to clean the wings,' said G.

My turning was improving but I still hadn't flown the aerotow or landed entirely on my own. G was in no hurry to rush things, handing over control judiciously. It was like starting all over again, which was good. But there was one thing that bothered me that I could not remember having felt before at Booker. I began to gain the impression that G was putting pressure on the rudder pedals in my turns, often in contradiction to my own. It seemed odd and I dismissed it from thought.

That evening I was surprised to discover that G had not been helping me with any of my turns while I was in control. This contradicted the sensation I had felt from the rudder pedals. Unlike the stick, which tends to centralise itself, the rudder needs to be pushed back into line or the airflow will keep it cocked. That was, evidently, the pressure I had felt on the rudder. 'Pressure,' explained G, 'is no clue to rudder position'.

Two flights were all I was to achieve that first day but I became an expert in logging and signalling, apart from two slips. 'Airfields are good places to make mistakes,' Terry had said. I was probably more interested in stopping the tea spilling as I crossed the runway towards the landing area. I looked up just in time to see a glider retract its air-brakes and whistle over my head. An angry fist shook.

The second incident occurred later that afternoon, when I was on the radio controlling a single-seater. On the All Out signal I noticed that the tow rope had slackened momentarily and seemed to be in danger of catching the wheel. I jabbed the mike: 'Stop'. The tug throttled back and the glider shot forward towards the tug's tail. 'Did I do right?' I enquired, defensively. In theory yes, I was told, but in practice the rope would have been fine. The woman in the gilder gave me a black look as they wheeled her back into position.

My log for the day read: 'Working on turning. Co-ordination. Work on lookout'. Lookout is important. The human eye is not good at distinguishing objects that are relatively stationary but excellent at detecting movement. Collisions occur when the relative bearing between two moving objects – two gliders, two supertankers – remains fixed, just the situation which the eye is not well equipped to distinguish.

A glider heading straight towards you is also extremely hard to detect. So why is it, I thought, that most gliders compound the problem by being white? Our K 13, like all the trainers I had so far flown, was painted red. Just as well. The trick to seeing tiny movements is to scan the horizon in a series of jerks. Some gliders have a blind spot behind and above.

———

Lasham Gliding Society's bar is a convivial place after a day's flying. Pilots are a friendly, approachable bunch and there was no trace of a 'them and us' complex. Everyone seemed equal – if not in ability then at least in their reasons for being on the airfield. I

Keeping a wary eye on a single-seater. The risk of collision in the air is highest when two gliders are approaching head-on and their profiles are the smallest. The situation is not made easier by the fact that most gliders are white, although some trainers have red wing-tips.

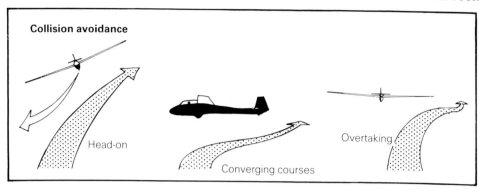

Collision avoidance

Head-on

Converging courses

Overtaking

was curious to know what kind of people decided to glide and, in particular, whether it was possible to speed up the learning process – say, by hiring an instructor exclusively for a week.

If I had the money, I asked Terry, could I book an instructor and learn to fly in a week? 'No. The gliding movement isn't run commercially. You can't buy an instructor – you have to take your place within the course structure. It's different in America, where you book your flight, turn up at the airfield and your glider is waiting for you. But it doesn't happen here. To learn you must join a course and take part in the general activities of the society. In any case it's the best way. There's more to gliding than just strapping in and taking off. It's important to learn airfield aware-ness and the waiting between flights is the best way to learn that. Anyway, four flights a day is enough for most people.'

A fellow novice called Phil introduced himself. Unlike me he had read all the books, could reel off the names of the parts and even knew the correct terms for the aerobatics we had witnessed taking place that afternoon above us.

Later, over an excellent steak and chips washed down by two pints of real ale, the four of us discussed *Gaia* physics, the theory that the earth is a living creature, capable of thought. Exhausting that topic, we retired to the video room and watched John Denver narrate a film about a Nevada gliding compe-tition. We followed it with a grainy archive film about early gliders, progressing from disastrous but enter-taining attempts in rudimentary flying machines, via Cayley and Otto Lilienthal and Percy Pilcher's early hang gliding experiments in the late 1890s, to the Wright Brothers and prewar German gliding.

In 1973 Lasham's own Derek Piggott had flown a replica of Cayley's 1863 glider in which the pioneer, then 80 and unable to fly himself, had persuaded his

A good look-out is only effective if there are rules to control action in the event of a potential collision. Head-on, turn right; converging courses, give way to glider on your right; overtaking aircraft, keep clear.

coachman to fly. Not surprisingly the coachman resigned soon after. I hadn't appreciated fully the impact the Germans had made on the sport in the prewar years, nor that gliding had been on the brink of being an Olympic sport when war intervened.

Germany is still responsible for building most of the world's gliders – not only our trusty K 13 but most of the top competition models – while Britain no longer makes any. Slingsby, whom until a few years ago produced a fine range of gliders, found the competition too stiff. Thus, of the 1,838 gliders registered with the British Gliding Association, the vast majority are foreign, and the list includes nearly 200 separate models. Only eight numbered more than 50 – the ASW 20, KA6cr and K6cr, Kestrel 19, Libelle std, Vega, Astir and our own K 13 (with 60). Gliders, like yachts, come in almost as many shapes as there are pilots to fly them.

Good second-hand gliders are not easy to find. A 12-year-old, reasonably high performance glider, a few of which were advertised at Lasham, was fetching £12-£14,000. Sharing between a syndicate of say, four, brings the costs down and is the most common form of ownership. Occasionally bargains can be found – like the beautiful, 16-year-old K 6 that turned up that weekend and bought without hesitation by its pilot for £4,500. He had found it in Switzerland and lovingly restored it to pass the strict Certificate of Airworthiness test that all British gliders must pass before they're allowed to fly.

Top competition gliders, and there are a number of categories – 15-metre, Open, and so on – can cost up to £30,000 and more for something like a Motor Janus which has an engine that pops out of the back of the fuselage for unassisted take-off.

As Phil and myself supped our beer and dreamed of soloing the idea of finding £3,000 each and forming a syndicate of our own didn't seem too far-fetched. I thought about the £4,000 I had a year before spent on the Honda 750 parked outside – and for which I still had two payments to complete. It was a question of commitment, literally with the sky the limit. Would there ever be a time when, not content with the odd weekend, I would join a syndicate and buy into a share of my own glider? Phil was definitely keen. 'OK,' I said. 'We'll all meet again here in five years' time – with our own gliders.'

'You're on,' responded Phil. 'The only difference is that I'll be flying in upside down, then perhaps I'll do a quick loop, sideslip and then land.'

I didn't doubt it.

DAY FIVE

G reat evil-looking black crows were strutting like fat friars on the grass below my window when the curtains drew back on another cloudless morning. Lasham has a comfortable if spartan bunk-house where I and half a dozen others on various courses were staying for the week. Living on the airfield allows you to put the outside world out of mind almost completely. Even newspapers were hard to come by unless you were prepared to drive a mile or so to the village.

Beyond the tarmac ribbon of the perimeter track, out across the curving green meniscus of the airfield, the wind was barely stirring the orange windsock on top of the satellite tracking station. Although it was only 8.30 two gliders were parked, wings down, beside the control bus. The early birds had been flying since 6.30.

On good days flying starts at first light when the air is stable, making it perfect for teaching courses. The gliders were K 13s, one of which had the rear half of its canopy blanked off to enable the pilot to learn instrument flying, which is used in clouds when the visibility often blanks out completely.

The biggest decision of the day was whether to wear my flying suit or not. Did nine flights entitle me to dress like a flying ace? No. I put on the jeans and T-shirt, had breakfast and wandered over to the hangars where Josef, a true ace Polish aerobatics instructor, was lending a hand in extracting ten tightly packed gliders. It was easy to see why so much of the damage inflicted takes place in or around the hangar.

Turning, co-ordinating stick and rudder, was to be the priority of the day. I'd been heartened to read Derek Piggott's experience about the use of rudder, for he agreed that the feet movements don't come naturally for the first few flights.

I had, incidentally, been wary of reading too much about gliding both before and during the course. It seemed better to learn first and then read later so as not to pre-empt anything that G would be about to teach. It's so easy to become a glider know-all without having any first-hand experience, but my ignorance about even very basic things was in sharp contrast to some of the others. Whether it was a help or whether a little reading would have hindered the learning process can be argued either way. My own experience suggests that it's better to do first and then *revise* later.

What I'd been reading, during the long hours on the airfield, was an account by an early flying pioneer, Sir Gordon Taylor, of his first experiences of flight, *The Sky Beyond*. Taylor, an Australian who had joined the Royal Flying Corps on the outbreak of war in 1914, had been thrown in at the deep end by a mad flying instructor who seemed intent of killing him before he had started. As an antedote to our own flying, where the sky was a pleasure dome, his was a world of lightning decisions where the penalties for slow reflexes were the stab of machine-gun bullets and the slow crippled spin towards quick death. It's worth quoting Taylor at some length:

" 'On the tarmac [the instructor] was perfectly friendly, even cordial, as we went out to the machine. But as soon as we were in our seats and our belts fastened he fired the engine and went off without any explanation or any indication of what we were going to do.

In the air we did a few gentle turns in which I had a somewhat indefinite part, not knowing really whether he, or I, was flying the aeroplane: a few minutes we were straight and level again; and then, with mixed emotions and a 'this is it' feeling, I realised that landings were on us.

This time I was told to do the landing – a shout from the front, with no details. I'd discovered that if you let the nose of this aeroplane go down beyond a certain speed you couldn't pull out; and that if you didn't put it down far enough it would stall and crash. So I took the controls and really concentrated on the critical action of keeping it in the correct glide, of easing her out, and touching the wheels down on the grass. I could feel the instructor sharing the controls, creating an uncertainty in opposition to my movements; and in this way we went on down, both landing the aeroplane. In some intangible fashion the landing turned out to be quite a good one – but I'd had enough. I was afraid and angry, and determined now to have a showdown with this man before another take-off.

He didn't give me a chance. To my utter astonishment he got up out of his seat, climbed over the side and down and stood on the grass of the aerodrome. Then he looked up and called to me, 'You can bloody well go solo now.'

For the moment the shock froze me into a state of inaction. I couldn't believe he was serious. Then he started to walk away. This was it. I had to make a decision, for better or worse. I put my hand over the side of the nacelle, felt for the switch, and stopped the engine.

The instructor turned and came back, shouting at me. 'What's the matter with you? Why did you stop the engine?'

Momentarily horror-stricken by the implications of my decision, I hit back at him. 'I'm not going solo!' "

Sir Gordon later won the Military Cross in the First World War and the George Cross for a daring exploit which involved climbing repeatedly out to the outboard engines of a flying-boat over the Tasman Sea, transferring oil from the tank of a failed engine to maintain the supply to the good engine.

––––––

My tenth flight saw nothing that dramatic, thank God. Taking control at the launch again I knew that G was poised to take over if things got badly out of shape; but until that happened, and I was determined that it should not, the movements were all my own. This time I flew a little too high on take-off, but managed to correct without crashing the wheel or skid back down on to the tarmac. I knew what I'd done and there was no need for G to tell me. He didn't.

Turns, turns, turns – and more bloody turns. This time I decided to fix on to the yaw string above my head, to control the stick and, especially, the rudder instinctively by watching the tuft of wool twitching. It didn't work. Rather than fly by the aspect of the nose, the horizon and the airspeed I became transfixed by the yaw string, following it and correcting rather than anticipating its movements. 'Good try,' said G, 'but don't rely on the yaw string. By the time it's moved you'll be out of position.'

The landing caught me unawares – probably something to do with my fixation for the yaw string. Before I'd fully registered what was going on the airfield was in sight and G was asking me to trim for 55 knots. At the final turn and airspeed was OK. Nose down and the runway ahead, I was all set to drive the glider deep into the turf at 70 knots when G called out, quietly, 'What sort of speed do you call that?'

'Seventy knots,' I replied, easing the stick back. That burst of speed, however, had ruined the carefully judged approach. Either we gave her full air-brakes now or it was going to be a longish walk back. Air-brakes out, we dropped to the ground, rounded out a little early and floated away towards parts unknown. As we were now flying closer to the stall speed, but high enough to damage ourselves if we stalled, G reduced the brakes a touch to bring down the stall speed and give a little time to sort things out – and we glided in to land.

'If you round out too early, or balloon, it's vital not to open the air-brakes again,' said G. 'The higher the speed of the glider the more air-brake you can safely use, and vice versa.

'The K 13's normal cruising speed is forty-two to forty-three knots. With full brake the minimum speed

'A perfect landing, but perhaps next time you could bring her in a little closer to the control bus,' thinks 'G' as his teaching glider is retrieved from some far-flung corner of Lasham's little empire.

OPPOSITE: A K 13 comes into land at Lasham, levelling out and showing the characteristic tail-down attitude as it rounds out for the final touchdown, air-brakes visibly out.

Air-brakes ruin the wings' lift by breaking the airflow over the top and bottom surfaces, causing the glider to sink. Spoilers on the top surface do the same, but to a lesser degree.

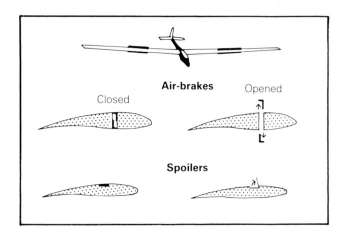

would be closer to fifty-five. With half-brake the minimum speed could be reduced to perhaps forty-eight knots and forty knots with no brake. We were doing about that when you rounded out too early, so it was better to let her lose height and speed naturally than risk a stall. And remember, whatever you do, don't push the stick forward to gain speed after an early round out – that will also result in a heavy landing. Remember the wind gradient effect as you get close to the ground.'

As I dragged the glider slowly back to the launch point I couldn't help reflecting that air-brakes were wonderful things. They seemed to be what the left hand is for. More than any other control they have an immediate and definite effect. Once you're aware of the danger of regarding them simply as landing levers their use comes naturally.

Their braking effect is secondary to their function in increasing the speed at which the glider stalls – in other words increasing the minimum flying speed. By deliberately sabotaging a significant part of the lifting surfaces of the wings and causing extra drag, the glider would need to be flown faster to counteract the loss of wing surface. Height loss is inevitable. Nevertheless the feeling of control they give is extremely satisfying, enabling the pilot to control precisely the point at which the glider will touch down; and, once down, they prevent it trying to fly again.

G's words began to make real sense. 'Don't fly it down. Just let the glider drop gently out of the sky and land itself when it's good and ready.'

As with most aspects of gliding, the use of brakes is a balancing act enabling the pilot to burn off excess height and control the approach angle. Overshooting is likely if the approach is too high and fast, under-

shooting if the speed and the glider are both too low. The use of brakes as landing levers in a low and slow situation, therefore, is potentially disastrous. Many more bad landings are made due to undershooting than overshooting. The juggling act that allows the pilot to land just where he wants, at the correct speed, with half air-brakes, is the essence of good landing – and once you've experienced the satisfaction of a good approach and round out the feeling is never forgotten.

Despite the presence of some weak thermals, flight

Air-brakes are what your left hand's for. They also break up the airflow over the wing, causing it to lose lift and thus allowing the pilot to control his rate of descent. Their function as brakes is limited, so a better name would be spoilers.

Using the air-brakes

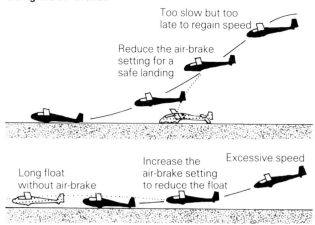

Too slow but too late to regain speed

Reduce the air-brake setting for a safe landing

Long float without air-brake

Increase the air-brake setting to reduce the float

Excessive speed

Air-brakes will cause the glider to stall at higher speeds, so it's essential to keep the speed up when using them to control the landing.

75

times were still too short at Lasham. A brief wrestle with the tug, a few turns and time to land. Flight 11 was to be no exception. By this time a strong cross-wind was blowing from left to right across the runway. Above the sky was hazy, and it was difficult to make out the horizon. Nevertheless the turns, while not second nature, were definitely improving. As we circled slowly in a small bubble of rising air it became clear that the ability to fly the glider efficiently is a vital part of using thermals. Bad turns burn up height due to the excess drag of the fuselage slipping or skidding through the air.

The turns were also being helped by a conscious decision to hold the stick less firmly. Thumb and forefinger were enough, allowing me to feel the glider's inherent balance. It was very like steering a well-balanced yacht.

Apart from a little help lining up the final turn, my landing was almost perfect. As the wind had now strengthened it was important to keep the speed up to avoid any chance of undershooting. Basically the stronger the headwind, the faster the approach should be made.

To illustrate the point you only have to take an extreme case. Say the wind was blowing at 50 knots at round out height and the glider's speed was also 50 knots, then the speed over the ground would be zero. The glider would be making no headway at all in relation to the ground and the dangers of undershooting would be high.

In a strong wind landing the final turn is made high and early and the approach is steep. Full brakes are used to burn off the height and, with judgment and practice, it's not difficult to make a spot landing. It's also always better to use full brake at once if height needs to be lost quickly than discover you need them later.

As I sat waiting my turn I thumbed the relevant chapter in Derek Piggott's *Gliding*. 'A common error is for the beginner to be far too cautious about opening the air-brakes, with the result that it becomes necessary to land with full air-brakes or run out of landing area altogether.'

Downwind landings are the reverse. As the wind is carrying the glider with it the ground speed will be equal to the glider's speed *plus* the wind speed. In this, extreme, case the ground speed would be 100 knots – clearly disastrous unless the field was the size of Heathrow and the glider could be allowed to float the required distance to burn off sufficient speed to make a safe landing. In practice flying would have been cancelled long before the wind had reached that speed, but landings in 25 knots of headwind are quite normal – as I was to discover the next day.

———

The last flight of this day was clearly influenced for the better by another chapter of *The Sky Beyond*. Here was a real pilot. Flying an overloaded Catalina and navigating only by sextant and compass, Gordon Taylor had just flown from Australia to Easter Island. As my name was called, Taylor had just blasted off towards South America. Reading his accounts of pioneering flights across uncharted waters put my little experiences into some sort of context.

Flight 12 was a good one. Again I had the sensation of doing everything more or less right without quite knowing why. The crosswind take-off and landing presented no problems, and was far less difficult than I'd imagined. Maybe it was because there was something to fight against, like the weather helm on a boat – a force to steer against rather than just the easy neutrality of the glider itself.

This time I avoided going too high on the aerotow and instead went a little too low, pulled back gently and swung into formation behind the tug. The transition was smooth. We even had time to discuss the merits of various fields if we were forced to make a landing out. G pointed out the fields where the crops were too high, and how the difference in colour within a field could mean that a fence that was invisible from the air lay between two different crops. Pathways and ditches are hard to spot from 2,000 feet but their

OVERLEAF: 'All out'... OK, start to lift her off, so far so good... whoops, a little more to the right, if you would... no, not too high, bring her down a little... that's better, level her out, watch the tug's wings... that's good, now concentrate. Phweew...

Approach the landing with extra speed when it's windy. The wind gradient effect, caused by ground friction, means that at low level the wind speed drops off and the glider's airspeed will be similarly reduced to the point where it might stall.

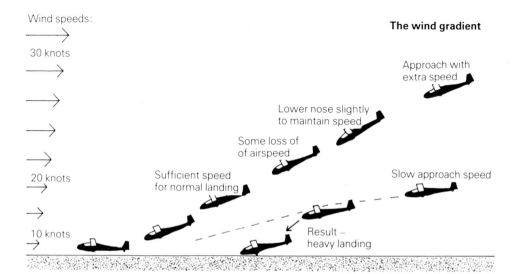

Wind speeds:

30 knots

20 knots

10 knots

The wind gradient

Approach with extra speed

Lower nose slightly to maintain speed

Some loss of of airspeed

Sufficient speed for normal landing

Slow approach speed

Result – heavy landing

presence can often be detected by changes in colour. All common sense, really.

———

Any pilot who trains at Lasham can hardly fail to be aware of the debt that the gliding movement owes to Derek Piggott. Until 1987 Piggott was the society's chief flying instructor, and although he's now semi-retired he still takes an active part in the running of the club. It was not long before I had a chance to meet him.

Derek was invited to become Lasham's chief flying officer in the year in which I was born, 1953. After a childhood spent making glider models he couldn't wait to join the RAF, where his natural aptitude made him one of the fastest learners they had ever trained. He spent the war in the RAF, training instructors at the Central Flying School and later testing troop-carrying gliders in India.

After the war he found himself in charge of ATC gliding and played an active part in setting up gliding in schools up and down the country, including my own. During a distinguished career spanning over 40 years, he has flown over 240 aircraft types, 160 of which have been gliders, including a number of prototypes. His flying time approaches 10,000 hours.

Derek is a fit-looking, bright-eyed man with those intense pilot's eyes and a precise manner of speaking. His recall is astonishing. His face lights up constantly at the memory of some long ago experience, whether it be the time he faced a rock wall in Turkey while testing a prototype light aircraft, or recounting the many films in which has had flown.

Derek has 'starred' in many of the flying films, from *Those Magnificent Men in their Flying Machines* to *The Blue Max*. He has flown Fokker triplanes, Camels, D7s, Spitfires and a number of specially constructed replicas, including a three-quarter scale SE5 which he designed from original plans. During his time in the RAF he also flew and instructed on many of the early jet-powered fighters, Vampires, Hunters and Meteors.

But it's as a glider pilot that his reputation is greatest. He developed many of the training methods now universally adopted, which place the emphasis on hand-on experience above classroom teaching. He's a great believer in letting the student get the feel for controlling the glider, reinforcing the learning process by debriefing rather than pre-flight lectures, much of which can be forgotten in the thrill of the moment.

Later, keen to learn more about this extraordinary man, I went to see him. I spent the best part of five hours at Derek's London house listening to his stories of flying, of the time he bailed out of a two-seater during an aerobatics competition when the cockpit canopy detached itself, demolishing the tail as it went, and of his exploits in early cloud flying. 'We used to head for the biggest cumulo-nimbus we could find just before the lightning strike,' he said. 'Flying totally blind – we couldn't even seen the wing-tips – we'd get sucked up to six thousand feet or more. Of course we now realise it's terribly dangerous. We'd have to check all the control wires and usually there would be some damage.'

Flying in thunder clouds is now banned following a tragic accident some years ago. No one knows what happened: the pilot may have lost control, or more likely the glider was blown apart by a massive strike. As we spoke he constantly looked out of the window at the pattern of clouds above. 'It becomes a habit. You're always watching the sky, always learning.'

The vast majority of his memories are happy ones – like the time at Lasham when, late one afternoon as they were packing up, he decided to fly the glider back to the hangar rather than drag it across the airfield. 'There was nothing visible from the ground. But at about fifteen hundred feet I felt the glider start to lift. The air was silky smooth. We just kept going up and up for four thousand feet as a sea breeze front came in. Marvellous, because it was quite unexpected.'

His obvious delight in flying has made Derek a contented if not wealthy man. At an age when most people are looking anxiously towards filling in their retirement time he's as active as ever. When I saw him last he was flying microlights and debating whether to take up hang gliding. 'The trouble when going from gliding to weight-transfer flight is that all the controls work in the exact opposite. To climb you pull back on the stick. In hang gliding you push the bar forward. Could be very confusing.' I had no doubt that the man who once flew an outrageously over-powered replica SE5 biplane upside-down before the engine cut out – for film director Blake Edwards in the film *Darling Lily* – would find hang gliding a piece of cake.

I left him setting off for Barnes Common to walk the family Labrador, but not before he had explained in great detail to me what the clouds were getting up to, three thousand feet above us.

DAY SIX

F ive days after that first flight at Booker nearly two years before, my total flying time was still only just under three hours – two hours and 43 minutes to be precise. That calculation was easy to make: the evidence was in the log-book. To gain those precious hours I'd spent 40 hours on the airfield, read five books and helped launch a hundred gliders.

There was little or no sense of frustration, however. By and large the weather had been fine, the company good and the time had passed easily enough. The deep satisfaction those few minutes in the air can give make up wonderfully for the hours of watching and waiting. No flight is too short not to learn at least something, or to leave its impression. Unless all glider pilots are blessed, miraculously, with instant recall, it cannot be a coincidence that all can relate the details of flights made many years previously. Perhaps that 'incredible thermal' has become even more incredible with the passing of time and that field landing a touch more hairy than it may in fact have been, but most of the facts remain surprisingly intact. And there is always someone at hand, who was up there at the same time, to put the facts right if they stray a little too far from what glider pilots regard as an acceptable approximation to the truth. In that they are not unlike fishermen.

Over and over again the golden rule was this: however unpromising the weather, it's always worth flying.

The previous evening, as we sat around the table with our log-books, filling in the details of each flight, I wondered how long it would be before I could go solo.

Of the four of us on the course Steve was probably the most experienced. Just under a year before he had gone solo after nearly 40 flights, but work and the difficulty in finding the time to go gliding had set him back. He was on the course to regain confidence in his own ability. Without regular flying practice confidence can drain away; everyday life is so risk-free that it's hard to remember what it's like to take your life in your hands.

Steve worked for Southampton City Council housing department. He was still finding difficulties in aerotowing and landing. It's a frustrating experience failing to do something that you know you can do, and in fact did do, once before.

John, on the other hand, had last been solo in 1947. Posted to Germany after the war he filled the boredom of army life by joining the local flying club. The instructors were all Luftwaffe pilots who, 18 months before, would have been flying Messerschmitts. 'They were tremendous pilots,' recalls John. 'Some of them were obviously a little resentful about us being there, but most were very friendly.'

John had learnt to fly in a 1935 Grunau Baby, a low-speed, lightweight German glider, eight of which are still listed on the BGA's records.

At the weekends perfect weather attracts pilots to Lasham from miles around. Queues can build up despite two winches and three aerotow tugs all working flat out to get the gliders airborne.

To have been in on gliding in the early days gave John a certain status among the younger members of the course. His original log-book had long since crumbled, but the details of those flights had been transferred to his new log-book and excited considerable curiosity from the instructors. John was recently widowed and had decided to go back to gliding after all those years to fill some of the time on his hands. Despite a slight weight problem which would, if he had so desired, prevented him from doing some of the more dramatic aerobatics, John was just one more of the untypical glider pilots I met during my week at Lasham.

Matthew, a medical writer, was already a member of a ridge soaring club in Staffordshire. Vastly experienced in winch launches, he'd booked a course here in order to learn aerotowing and, perhaps, go solo at the end of the week. Lasham instructors believe in taking things slowly. Neither Steve nor Matthew were to get the chance, but both were close. The difference between flying the glider yourself, knowing there's an instructor behind you, and going up on your own may be purely a psychological barrier, but it's no less strong.

———

In the early days of gliding the gentle approach was simply not possible. Delays and frustration have always been a part of gliding. The early pioneers not only risked life and limb but also had to repair their flimsy craft after each painful descent. As well as learning to fly they were also learning how to make a glider fly, and often learning too how to make and repair the gliders they flew. Trial and error in equal proportion was the only way.

The history of early flight is, not surprisingly therefore, littered with diaster. But when exactly was that first flight made, and by whom? Modern flight may have started with Sir George Cayley, Otto Lilienthal and the Wright Brothers, but man's desire to emulate the birds stretches back much further.

The first man credited with attempting heavier-than-air flight was Daedalus. Having constructed the mythical Cretan Labyrinth, the local ruler King Minos, understandably reluctant to lose such a distinguished engineer, imprisoned Daedalus and his son Icarus in a high tower. Proving that necessity was the mother of invention, they decided to escape by constructing a glider from eagle feathers and beeswax. The legend goes that the young Icarus, intoxicated by the sensation of what must have been the

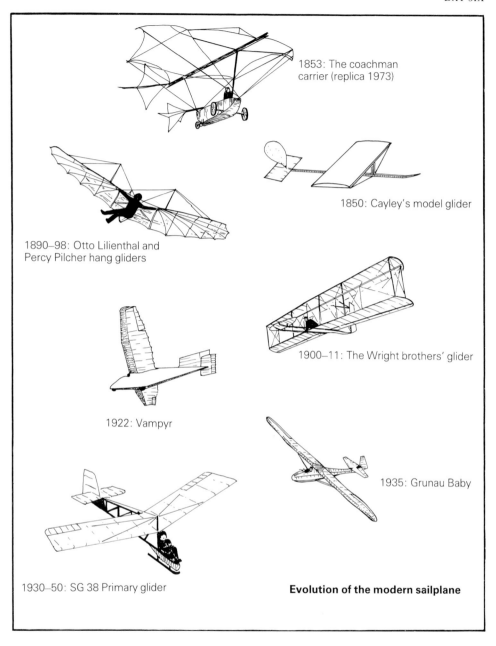

1853: The coachman carrier (replica 1973)

1850: Cayley's model glider

1890–98: Otto Lilienthal and Percy Pilcher hang gliders

1900–11: The Wright brothers' glider

1922: Vampyr

1935: Grunau Baby

1930–50: SG 38 Primary glider

Evolution of the modern sailplane

first recorded example of thermalling, soared too high; the heat of the sun melted the wax and he fell to his death. What's not often realised is that his father went on to make a copybook landing.

Like most myths there must have been an element of truth in the story. Some years ago an attempt was made by a group from MIT (Massachusetts Institute of Technology) to reconstruct that flight and their pedal-powered craft, with a wingspan of over 100

The shape of the glider as we know it today evolved between the world wars, primarily in Germany.

feet, flew successfully for over 70 miles, crash-landing in a welter of Kevlar and cling-film on the coast of Greece.

Nothing much happened, or at least little has come down to us, of subsequent attempts at flight after the Greeks. The story of Icarus was handed down not only as a terrible warning to the overkeen in general, but to the overkeen birdman in particular. Daedalus, through the help of the gods, no doubt, had got away with trespassing in an element alien to man, but the lesson was clear.

We next hear of flight from the manuscripts of venerable monks, who seem to have been forever tinkering with ideas to relieve the tedium of *te deums* and the monastic life as a whole. When they got boared with beekeeping, it appears, they turned their attentions to the skies, and the high towers of medieval Christendom were a magnet for the early pioneers of flight. A paper in the January 1983 Journal of the Royal Aeronautical Society lists nearly 50 attempts in early heavier-than-air flying machines between 850 BC and 1783; half of these seem to have been made from the towers of abbeys, churches and castles.

One of these stories concerns Eilmer, a Benedictine monk at Malmesbury Abbey in Wiltshire. In 1020 he was said to have jumped off one of the high towers attached to a pair of wings and succeeded in flying down the main street, landing in front of the town cross. This is clearly the first example of a glider pilot tall story. It's far more likely that he simply floated down almost vertically, landing under the walls of the abbey, where he was scraped up and his two broken legs were attended to. The account of the flight first appeared in a medieval manuscript written some years later by Abbott William of Malmesbury, entitled *De Gestis Anglorum*. Visitors to Malmesbury today can purchase a leaflet relating the story, if they so wish.

Most of the flights listed in the RAS Journal, including those by John Damian at Stirling Castle and John Williams at Conway, were probably no more than wing-assisted landings, more relevant to the history of parachuting than gliding. Certainly the experiments by Cayley and Lilienthal were conducted more in the quest for powered flight than gliding, for at that time little was known about the existence of thermals.

Cayley, who lived near Scarborough, was aware of the lifting properties of aerofoils and by 1804 had evolved the modern layout with tailplane and fin from his experiments with model gliders. Progressing from models, Cayley was soon constructing very much larger machines, ballasted first with lead or stones then with animals and finally, in a memorable flight at Brompton Dale in 1853, when Cayley was 80 and unable to fly himself, with his coachman aboard the craft. The controls were lashed to prevent the unfortunate man hastening the inevitable and once on the ground he took immediate steps to rid himself of a master whose demands, even in the absence of trade unions, would have been regarded as definitely above and beyond the call of a normal chauffeur's duties.

Derek Piggott's flight in a replica of the 'coachman glider' in the making of a television documentary was one of the high points of his career. Not only did he have to make a number of flights in the machine – which looked like a bird carrying a bath-tub – but simulate the final crash. 'It flew in a fashion,' he told me with a twinkle in his eye at the memory.

Otto Lilienthal took things a stage further, or at least more successfully, but most of his flights were made in rudimentary hang gliders, shifting his weight to change direction rather than in the forerunner of the gliders flown today with controlled surfaces. Lilienthal's knowledge of aerofoils was nonetheless extensive at the time of his last flight, when he crash-landed and was killed.

From then on the quest for powered flight overshadowed the development of gliders until shortly after the First World War. The Versailles Treaty had banned Germany from creating an air force, but the great advances made during the war were too exciting not to be pursued in some form. The ingenious Germans soon found a loophole in the treaty by flying gliders – which meant that at the outset of the Second World War their pool of glider pilots and knowledge of aerodynamics catapulted them to an early air superiority. By the 1920s gliders were already flying for hours rather than minutes and the sport of soaring was established in many countries.

Most soaring relied on the effective harnessing of wind blowing over ridges creating an updraft (even in moderate winds) of about 600 feet per minute. The machines were light with a large wing area, and consequently slow, rather like a modern hang glider. In light winds the only way to reduce the gliding angle was to increase the efficiency of the wing, improve the lift and cut out as much drag as possible.

Derek Piggott, in his book *Understanding Gliding*, explains the theory better than this pilot: 'It is not difficult to produce a satisfactory hill-soaring machine unthought of tolerances while keeping the wing weight as low as possible.'

The new sections, however, were immediately successful, giving an improved gliding angle and better aileron control. The lessons learned in wing design soon influenced fuselage shapes; fuselages matter of building a very light machine with a large wing area – ie, having a low wing loading. The weight of the wing structure can be kept very low if it is wire- or strut-braced. This could have a serious drag penalty at high speed but for normal hill soaring at low speed the extra drag is not sufficient to affect the soaring performance significantly.'

The quest for efficiency meant somehow losing those struts and wires and finding another method to keep the wings rigid and twist-free. As glider pilots began to discover the existence of thermals, searching for lift under the rain clouds that would appear from time to time over hill-soaring sites, the need for faster gliders, in which they could seek out pockets of lift, became even greater.

A low rate of sink became less important than speed and the thick aerofoils used on low speed hill-soaring machines were gradually replaced by thinner sections. Struts and wires gave way to the D-box, whereby the first third of the wing was in the form of a rigid box to resist the twisting forces on the wing. 'These perhaps did not produce quite so much lift at low speeds,' wrote Derek Piggott, 'but they had far less drag when the glider was flown with extra speed against the wind or through sinking air between thermals.'

Faster speeds aggravated the problems of landing in confined spaces. Film of early hill soaring shows gliders side slipping in to land to reduce speed and increase the rate of descent. Air-brakes and spoilers were the next development.

By the outbreak of the Second World War the best machines were achieving glide ratios of about 1:30 – that is, losing one foot of height for every 30 feet flown forward. Gliding as a sport virtually ceased during the war, but development was rapid from 1945 onwards. Wind tunnel testing on fighter-plane wings had produced increasingly efficient aerofoils. The problem was, however, how to manufacture accurate sections light enough for a glider to benefit.

'In order to maintain the necessary smoothness,' explains Derek, 'the ply skin of the torsion box had to be extended back over most of the wing. The spacing of the supporting ribs had also to be closed up to prevent the plywood sagging. Most importantly, the contours of the whole wing had to be built to hitherto for use in strong wind conditions. Since the rate of sink is proportional to both the gliding angle and the flying speed, an acceptably low sink rate may be obtained just by making the glider fly slowly, even if the gliding angle is relatively poor.

'A low flying speed,' writes Piggott, 'is largely a became streamlined and pilots were forced to adopt a reclining position to maximise the advantages.

Even today the developments continue as designers discover better ways of using modern materials to create wing profiles that offer the best compromise between high speed and lift. Flaps are now incorporated into the trailing edges in order to change the profile to give either high speed or better lift, depending on the requirements of the glider pilot. Water ballast – a strange idea for those who think gliders should be as light as possible – enables the pilot to achieve a better air penetration and higher speeds into the wind by increasing the wing loading. The water can just as easily be jettisoned at a later stage, although it takes a skilled pilot to decide exactly when that moment as arrived. There are no taps in the skies with which to refill the depleted tanks.

Nevertheless, the perfect glider has yet to be designed. Many factors need to be taken into account, and everything is a matter of compromise. Gliders do have one significant advantage over most other forms of transport in that they are operating for most of the time, apart from landing and taking off, in only one element: air. Unlike a yacht, which operates half in

Wind blowing up the face of a hill can produce perfect conditions for soaring.

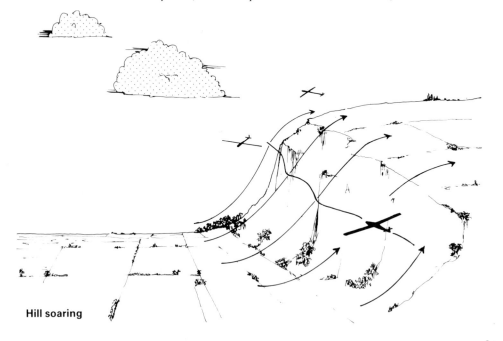

Hill soaring

A relatively high-performance Astir cs, with retractable nose wheel and shaped to provide the least resistance to the oncoming airflow. Like a submarine, but working in air, the glider is one of the most beautiful of man's creations, capable of staying aloft almost indefinitely in the right conditions.

and half out of the water, a glider is totally enclosed by air; only on landing does it have any sort of interface between air and earth.

In this respect the glider is much more like a submarine. Both are the purest shapes capable of carrying what they are designed to carry. Both exhibit the same features of simple, unsuperfluous efficiency that unite both designers and casual observers in admiration.

The credentials of a perfect glider are not difficult to list, but in practice they are hard to produce. A shape efficient for one set of conditions is usually hopeless for another, as Derek Piggott explains: 'In order to use thermals efficiently the glider must have easy handling and good control so that it can be manoeuvred quickly into the centre of the lift. It must also have a low rate of sink at low speeds in order to use small weak thermals. A low speed gives a small radius of turn and is frequently the key factor which determines whether a particular type of glider can stay up in difficult soaring conditions. However, in cruising flight between areas of lift it needs a flat gliding angle at high speed and, of course, at the end of the flight it must be easy to land in a confined space.

'Good low-speed performance for thermalling is best obtained by having a low wing loading, since the wing loading determines the minimum flying speed, and the radius of turn is proportional to the speed.

However, good performance at high speed is easiest to obtain with a high wing loading since it increases the speed for the best gliding angle.

'If the lift is strong, the glider with a high wing loading will average a much higher speed, in spite of climbing less efficiently. However, if the lift is very weak it might be unable to climb at all and the extra wing loading is a definite disadvantage.'

Most modern, high-performance gliders get round this problem, as I explained briefly earlier, by carrying water which increases the wing loading for fast flight in strong lift, but can be jettisoned when the lift is weak to reduce the rate of sink. The difficulty comes when the glider has jettisoned the ballast, then finds strong lift and needs, once again, to fly fast.

Flaps are the alternative to carrying water ballast. They change the shape of the wing itself in flight, like a bird – a fatter aerofoil for slow flight, thinner for fast flight. Flaps come in the form either of leading edge or trailing edge flaps. Unlike ballast, which increases the wing loading for faster flight, flaps change the shape of the wing, thus altering the flying characteristics. Yet they can be returned to their previous shape at the pull of a lever. The problem is one of engineering: 'The wing area may be increased by extending wing flaps for circling flight in the thermals, and reduced again by retracting them for efficient high-speed flight between thermals. However, this is not easy to do

Gliders all break down into component parts for ease of trailing. This high-performance Ventus can be assembled and disassembled in about half an hour. In addition to ailerons it has flaps, clearly seen on the right-hand wing. These alter the wings' lifting characteristics – more curved for high lift thermalling or flatter for fast flight.

without incurring drag losses which more than offset the advantages gained.'

This all plays little part in those early flights. The closest we came to mentioning flaps was during that initial CB SIFT CB check. The thought of yet another lever to push, on top of all those I had been called upon to use, was a little intimidating – quite apart from the idea of carting around gallons of water.

In fact, to return to reality, six days into my gliding career my log-book had barely filled half a page. Three hours it may have been, but my flights of fantasy could have filled a dozen or more. G had written after the last day's flying: 'Another day on basic turning. Big improvement on the last flight and a good landing in crosswind.' Just as he had predicted, things were beginning to happen unconsciously. I was not so much thinking as doing.

———

The third day at Lasham dawned fine again and I slept late, surfacing at breakfast long after the gliders had been dragged from their hangar. The weather had been steadily improving over the week and today was predicted to be a good one for thermals.

A knowledge of basic meteorology is not considered essential for a novice glider pilot, but clearly important later on. Cross-country flights depend on developing a nose for rising air and the best glider pilots use a hundred tiny indicators, literally smelling

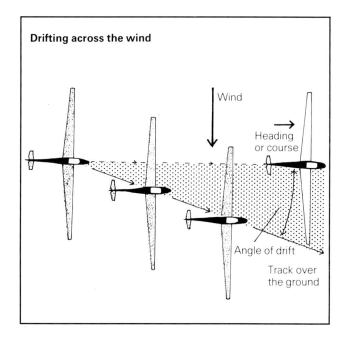

Drifting across the wind

Wind

Heading or course

Angle of drift

Track over the ground

The glider may be pointing straight ahead but, like a yacht stemming a cross-tide, the track over the ground will reflect the wind direction.

out the draughts of air as they bubble off the land. The smoke of chimneys or burning stubble rising, often carrying little bits of straw, birds circling and the formation of cumulus clouds are three of the obvious signs of lift.

In most countries a good thermal day follows immediately after the passage of a cold front, ahead of an area of high pressure, and there are tables that give the conditions likely to produce lift based on factors like dew point, temperature, wind direction and a dozen others. But there seems, in the last analysis, to be no substitute for that sixth sense a pilot develops for sniffing out the presence of thermals.

For the novice the thought of keeping a lookout for thermals while you are still wrestling with controlling the glider, especially when there are no obvious signs, is too much to handle at one time. Clearly the ability to spot thermals comes with experience.

Visible or not their presence, even on a training flight, is exhilarating, signifying free air time. To be towed to 2,000 feet and ten minutes later find the altimeter reading 3,000 feet is like finding a fiver in the pocket of an old coat. The question then is whether you spend it all at once or eke it out over as long a period as you can.

As my turns were getting much smoother now it was possible to indulge in a little thermalling. Holding the stick lightly, keeping a good lookout for other gliders racing in to join us in the bubble, we circled slowly, banking into the lift, feeling the rising air on the inside wing-tip.

The normally calm voice in the back changed, and instructor was now pilot again. My clumsy attempts to keep the glider flying in the area of maximum lift must have been frustrating for G. While I could see and feel virtually nothing, he was alive to every subtle change in altitude, calling me into the turns with increasing excitement. 'OK, turn to the left. Steeper or we'll lose it. That's it, keep the turns steady. No, we're losing it. We're in bad sink now, can you feel it? No, we've lost it . . .' and so on, until it was clearly time to look for the airfield.

The presence of thermals is like a magnet to other gliders. There you are circling merrily in your own little bubble when suddenly you are aware of gliders fanning in from all directions to join you. As it's hard to spot a glider coming at you head on, a good lookout is essential. Moreover, as the rate of climb varies from glider to glider there's no guarantee that the stack or 'gaggle' will stay in the same order as that invisible column sucks you up towards the cloud base.

Soon there may be 30 gliders gyrating beneath and above you, milking the lift of every foot before finally peeling off and heading off towards another likely spot. Thermals bubble off like well-timed geysers, popping up in sequence like champagne corks at a reception. When one has gone it's time to circulate towards another bottle for the next top-up.

The decision when to break off soaring depends on height and distance from the landing-place. I was told never leave it too late to make a safe circuit and landing. Thermals naturally move with their clouds with the wind, taking the glider downwind with them. Beating back gainst the wind with too little height can leave the pilot no option but to sample the nearest convenient field. Different clubs have their own rules, but normally 600 feet is the limit at which the pilot must break off thermalling and head for home, although he or she is warned never to rely on the altimeter on the final approach.

'Trim to 55,' said the voice from behind. 'Landing checks.' The 13th landing of my flying career would have been a cracker. By this time the technique of holding the stick lightly had become almost natural.

Cumulus clouds signal the presence of thermals, invisible bubbles of rising air.

In Australia they say FUST, in New Zealand SUFB. In Britain it's usually UFSTAL – Undercarriage, Flaps, Speed, Trim, Air-brakes, Lookout. Of all these, speed

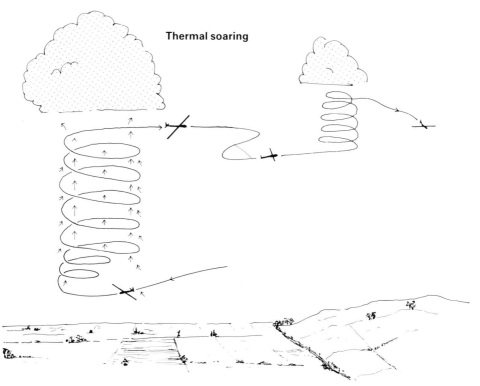

Thermal soaring

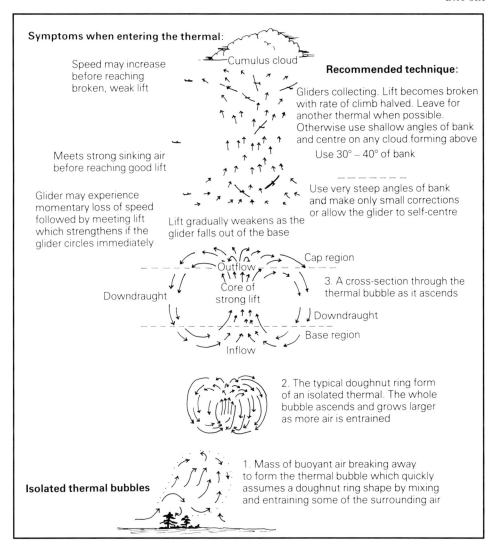

Symptoms when entering the thermal:

Speed may increase before reaching broken, weak lift

Cumulus cloud

Recommended technique:

Gliders collecting. Lift becomes broken with rate of climb halved. Leave for another thermal when possible. Otherwise use shallow angles of bank and centre on any cloud forming above

Use 30° – 40° of bank

Meets strong sinking air before reaching good lift

Glider may experience momentary loss of speed followed by meeting lift which strengthens if the glider circles immediately

Lift gradually weakens as the glider falls out of the base

Use very steep angles of bank and make only small corrections or allow the glider to self-centre

Outflow — Cap region

Downdraught

Core of strong lift

Downdraught

3. A cross-section through the thermal bubble as it ascends

Base region

Inflow

2. The typical doughnut ring form of an isolated thermal. The whole bubble ascends and grows larger as more air is entrained

Isolated thermal bubbles

1. Mass of buoyant air breaking away to form the thermal bubble which quickly assumes a doughnut ring shape by mixing and entraining some of the surrounding air

is probably the most important, although it's not a bad idea to look where you're going to make sure you're not about to alight on a row of gliders.

It's also normal to check for loose items in the cockpit that might interfere with the controls. During a long cross-country flight the pilot may have maps, pencils, calculators and the remains of his lunch rattling around in the cockpit as he prepares to land, any one of which can cause a distraction or problem.

As the final turn approached I concentrated on looking over the nose, not down beyond at the airfield swinging towards me. Rather than rudder in towards the landing area the turn was just like any other. The airfield swam into a view as the glider banked steeply

The anatomy of a thermal is complex and demands skill from the pilot if he's to milk it to its full.

to the right and the wings levelled; it was time to pick an aiming point, controlling the descent with the air-brakes.

Would we never touch down? G held open the brakes and the glider floated off down the airfield. As the glider's tail-wheel finally hit the grass I was so surprised the stick jumped forward from between my thumb and forefinger. We weren't going anywhere.

The elation of landing comprises two parts. First, the relief of being safely down, especially if you have any lingering fears of flying, as I did. Second, the satisfaction of getting down not so much in one piece but with style. Eyes are ever alert on an airfield to faults. You may make any cock-up you like way above in the privacy of your Perspex bubble, but the landing, like the docking of a yacht, is often a very public affair. And to add to your own sense of inadequacy there are the remarks of the recovery crew to endure as you step guiltily from the cockpit half a mile down the airfield.

The landing, in this case, had been good. G had held her off by regulating the air-brakes long enough to prove the point that the glider will eventually, when it has burned off speed, land itself.

Terry Joint brings a K 13 into land using side slip to burn off height. The altimeter reads from just under 300 feet to 100 feet, but the airspeed is lower than it would be if the pilot were using air-brakes. In the first picture it seems to be stuck on zero as the glider crabs sideways, before picking up to 50 knots on the final approach and just under 40 for the landing.

I was beginning now to be much more aware of the airfield and the steps needed to bring the glider into the circuit and the plan of the approach and final turn, though it would be some flights yet before I was called on to make the decisions necessary. I must say I was also a little relieved that my 13th flight was now behind me ...

———

The last flight of the day brought much of what I had learned so far together. The presence of thermals had prolonged both flights enough to allow us to enjoy the sensation of 'flying on empty'. The end always came too soon, but for a while it was just possible to imagine what it was like being up on your own.

The aerotows were coming along well. They still held the most fear. I was beginning to regard them as the necessary price to be paid for gliding, both literally and metaphorically. Whereas most of the sensations in gliding are relatively gentle – even the landing is a precise, controlled event – the aerotow, or winch launch, is a fairly brutal affair. There's something unnatural about being dragged into the sky behind a straining engine, and the transition is sudden and irreversible. Once the nose lifts off there's no going

A K13 at 200 feet climbs over the Dan Air repair hangars at the start of its aerotow. The airspeed is about 60 knots and rate of climb +8. The yaw string is flying straight, showing that the fuselage is meeting the airflow head on with least resistance.

back – no way of saying, 'OK, that's it. Let's stop this now before it gets out of hand.'

Then, because the glider is moving from rest to 70 or so knots in such a short time, the controls go from being crude to highly sensitive in seconds.

All was fine until about 500 feet, and then I lost it. '*OK, I have control,*' said the calm voice from the back, and immediately the oscillation stopped. I could feel the controls moving with the precise urgency of an experienced pilot. It was again instructive to put a hand on the stick, feet on the pedals and lightly feel the co-ordination at work from behind me.

At 2,000 feet the tow-rope bounced away, we levelled into steady flight and I was invited to take control. Stalls were again on the menu, but now they held no terror. G would bring the nose up until the buffeting started, until there was nowhere for the stick to go, hard back on the seat between my legs. '*Now recover!*' Stick forward, pick up speed, round out and back to level flight. No problem.

As we walked back to the clubhouse Josef and his pupil were performing an aerial ballet above us, doing all the things we'd been told not to do. Spins, climbing turns, chandelles and finally flying along upside-down. I could just make out their white sun-hats, 1,500 feet up over Lasham. Hmm, one day . . .

DAY SEVEN

I had gone to bed with *The Sky Beyond* and awoke to another glorious morning. Sir Gordon had been climbing from the cockpit of a Spitfire, surely one of the most beautiful aircraft ever built and about as far removed from our K 13 as it would be possible to imagine. The date was 1950. Sir Gordon was back in Australia at the RAAF field at Richmond, transfixed by the sight of a Spitfire standing on the grass by the runway...

" 'Would you like to fly it?' said the CO.

Now I was confronted with this light and wonderful aircraft, charged with the terrific power of the Rolls-Royce Merlin engine, not only available to my hand but necessarily to be controlled quite accurately by its movements. I could not, of course, decently escape from the invitation to fly this formidable single-seater fighter. This, and the exciting attraction of being free in the air with all this horsepower in an aircraft that could be so lightly handled, relieved me of any too visible hesitation in accepting the invitation to fly it.

We strolled over to the Spitfire and I climbed into the cockpit, close and intimate with all the controls and instruments concentrated in so small a space. Keeping as easy a manner as I could, I turned and suggestively asked the CO, standing beside me on the wing, 'Could you show me the knobs?' 'Oh, yes, of course,' he replied casually.

Brushing lightly over my ignorance in an attempt to

meet his manner without appearing to be too con-
cerned, I nevertheless mentally recorded certain
things I positively wanted to know before I unleashed
this concentrated source of power and committed
myself to control it in the air . . .

We started the engine, and the Spitfire came to life.
My host dropped down from the wing and I was alone
with the most terrific impression of latent power I
have ever known in an aeroplane. It was like sitting in
the streamlined rear of a powerful engine installation
removed from the wing of a large aircraft and placed
upon an undercarriage; with small, rigid wings
sprouting from the undersides of the cowl. The
dominant factor was the Rolls-Royce Merlin, with its
gigantic propeller. The aeroplane itself, the Spitfire,
with perfect manners and understatement of its own
significance, seemed merely the streamlined accom-
paniment to the engine. It seemed ridiculous that the
small throttle lever could control such power . . .

I fed the power with the throttle and she took me
away with violent acceleration, drawing my head
back against the rest, and hurrying quickly for flight
. . . Climbing to the freedom of the high sky I poured
her down again with the wild song of speed; drew her
up again, laughing, for the sky; and over off the top, to
touch the air with momentary surprise in level flight
. . . This was living. This was the aeroplane which
inspired John Gillespie Magee, the young Canadian
fighter-pilot, to write *High Flight* . . .' "

What that had to do with Lasham on a cool spring
morning I had only a vague idea, but I found the
reading of it inspirational. In some way it placed me
within the totality of the flying experience. I may
never fly a Spitfire, but I'd be flying in the same air.
And if I ever did fly a powered aircraft I would be
more aware of the forces.

Derek had explained to me that glider pilots,
because they are constantly alert to the changing
patterns of weather and the subtle fluctuations in
thermal activity, are far more in tune with their
environment than pilots of powered aircraft. 'In a
glider you're constantly having to make decisions that
the pilot of a powered aircraft, who can choose at will,
is seldom called upon to take,' he said.

Although glider flying isn't part of a normal flying
course, glider pilots, while not necessarily faster
learners, usually make better pilots in the long run.
There was no justification in thinking that we were
'poor relations' or that what we were doing was any
less challenging than flying a 'real' aeroplane.

By the time I had 'slipped the surly bonds of Earth'

Lasham's control bus is the nerve centre of the launching process. The triple lights are flashed in sequences to signal to the winch driver, a mile upwind, when the glider is ready to be launched. Winch launching is cheaper than aerotow but limited to about 1,500 feet.

the morning had gone. Cumulus, like puffs of cannon smoke, were drifting across an otherwise flawless May sky. This would be the day, I thought, to put everything into practice. Sir Gordon had taken me up the night before in one of the most awe-inspiring fighters of the Second World War. The K 13 would be a piece of cake.

Resisting the temptation to don my flying suit I clambered into the front seat of the glider, ran through the checks and fixed my eyes on the broken white lines on the tarmac until they disappeared over the curve of the field into the green backdrop beyond Lasham village.

Placing both hands lightly on the stick I waited for the tug to drop into the field, taxi round and line up. 'Are we all clear above and behind?' There was minute's pause while a K 13 leapt into the air to our left. 'Take up slack'. The tug's engines picked up, the rudder waggled the fuselage into alignment. 'All out'. The pitch of the engine rose, the rope tightened, pulling the nose forward once in a little jerk, slackened and then took the strain as we scraped and bounded into the air, feeling the wings bite, hold and lift, correcting the drift with short, sharp stabs of opposite rudder until the smooth movement of flight was established.

Wings perfectly level in the steady air, the glider vaulted the boundary hedge at about 300 feet, strain-

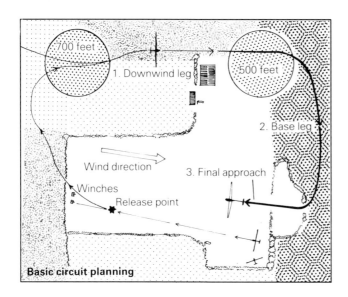

Basic circuit planning

The classic circuit plan, showing the stages of descent and where the glider should be positioned.

ing upwards into the slipstream flowing off the aircraft ahead. For a minute the nose never wavered, matching the movements of the tug stick for stick, rudder for rudder.

At 1,800 feet we began to meet patches of milky haze. The tug had stopped climbing and was banking gently back towards the airfield. 'We'll be going into cloud if you don't release,' said G. 'What's your height?' I tapped the altimeter, trying to make sense of the figures. Before I knew it the glider's nose had dropped fractionally and I found myself staring up at the tug's tailplane.

The momentary loss of concentration was enough. I jerked the stick back and to the left and in trying to get back in line I let the tug drift round to the right. The tow-rope took up a deep bow. Before it had jerked tight again G had the controls.

The cloud was thickening around us, partly obscuring the tug, and we released a little early before losing sight of the tug altogether. Two pulls on the toggle, a steep bank to the left, and then level.

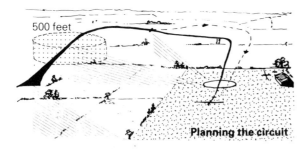

Planning the circuit

The angle at which the airfield appears under the wing is the best way of judging distance and height. The glider turns into its base leg at 500 feet before the final turn and approach.

'Air-brakes to get us out of this cloud. Watch the tug,' said G as the Rallye appeared high and to our right.

The brakes bit and the glider detached itself from the cloud base, circling away from the tug which had levelled out and down for the landing, away to the right behind us.

At 1,500 feet we levelled out. 'I want you to keep practising those turns,' said G. 'This time I want you to bank left, straighten up and bank right, all in one smooth movement.' For the next few minutes I tried to do just that – to swing the glider left and smoothly right without a break in the rhythm.

But there was no time to repeat the turning mantra. Unless it happed instinctively, it wouldn't happen at all. Once the rhythm was found, the glider became an extension of my body, reacting naturally to the movements of stick and rudder as if hands and feet had been waiting since childhood for this moment.

My reveries were brought to a swift close as usual by the need to position for the landing.

The end of the airfield lay to our right, 700 feet below as we made our way downwind, turned above the storage tanks that had become the reference point for the base leg and set up the approach for 55 knots.

An imaginary line across from the white strips at the end of the tarmac runway was to be the aiming point. As the air-brakes brought us down to what the other instructor described as 'the height of two elephants' we rounded out and came to rest. 'We'll make a glider pilot of you yet,' said the compliment-ary voice from the back.

———

Yet with eight of our flights completed and two more to go it was looking increasingly unlikely that I would be allowed to go solo. The best I could aim for would be an unassisted take-off, flight and landing. There was nothing now that I had not done, so it was simply a question of bringing it all together. Both Steve and Matthew were on the brink of solo and it was easy to see their impatience.

Two more flights that day would be enough to iron out most of the rough spots and a couple on Friday to put it all into practice. My total flying time had crept up to three hours and 22 minutes. The longest fights, 28 and 23 minutes, had been the day before.

Thermalling high about Hampshire I had not wanted to come down. If there had been any way to keep the glider up I would have taken it. To practise stalls on a day like that had seemed criminal; to waste

so much precious height when all the glider wanted to do was soar seemed tragic. But there was always the thought of the others waiting on the ground for their turn.

The 16th flight of my gliding career came and went. A good aerotow from start to finish, more stalls, more turns, a gentle descent and spot-on landing. Flight 17 was equally satisfying and if I hadn't managed to get so out of shape on the final stages of the aerotow it might even have qualified for a first ever 'hands on' flight from beginning to end.

By now I should have had the measure of the

A single-seater is whisked into the sky by winch, with the winch truck at the far end of the runway. The parachute which deploys once the glider has detached itself to bring the wire gently down to earth can be seen just ahead of the glider's nose.

Terry Joint prepares to give the 'Take up slack' signal once his helper has finished checking that the aerotow ring is attached to the nose hook. This more modern K 13 has a nose wheel instead of the older skidded model.

aerotow. If it still came hard, at least I knew what I was doing wrong, and the 600-foot mark seemed to be the crucial time. Just as I had relaxed a little from the initial concentration, a slight deviation would send the glider lurching off either to the left or right and too much correction only aggravated the problem.

The air was also becoming more turbulent above the airfield which did not help, but I knew that unless I could control the aerotow in all conditions there was little likelihood of achieving my goal by the end of the day. As soon as I landed I wanted to get up there again and prove that I could do it – or else suggest that we spend longer on the tow, which I knew was not possible.

Steve was into full spins and recoveries by this time. Matthew, in his sure, steady way, was hoping to solo by the end of the course. Both were having no problems with the aerotow.

———

At that moment we were due for a rude interruption. Just after I'd landed a red Land-Rover with flashing lights sped into view along the perimeter track, the signal that a Dan Air flight was about to land. Somewhere to the north of us a Boeing 737 was waiting for use to clear our flimsy little gliders off the runway. It was like waiting for a hurricane.

Over the radio we could hear the pilot calling Dan

Air control, his voice betraying little of the impatience he must have been feeling. Suddenly our little world seemed threatened. The hard reality of commercial flying was about to intrude on the tranquillity of the Hampshire countryside.

We scuttled for cover, dragging the gliders to the safety of the perimeter. The Boeing came sweeping round over the horizon, trailing lines of thin dirty smoke, lined up low over the trees and, thundering in over the boundary, touched down with a puff of smoke that left the smell of rubber clinging to the air.

There are strict rules about flying gliders in the vicinity of jet aircraft. The swirling vortices from the wings of a commercial airliner can disturb the air behind it for some minutes, spreading turbulence along a wide swathe. To attempt to land a glider soon after a jet would be to court disaster.

————

That evening we supped pints and talked of flying. 'I think I'm at the stage when, if someone threatened to kill my sister unless I went solo, I probably could,' I said to Phil, the New Zealander with the unending supply of jokes.

'I don't know about that,' he replied, 'but I reckon I'm at the stage now when, if someone threatened to cut off my finger, I definitely could.' Actually what he said was much more rude.

Above our heads a single-seater was putting on an aerial display of dazzling aerobatics. The turns were so controlled, the loops, spins and chandelles so graceful that we stopped drinking to watch.

When the glider had landed a slight, blonde woman unbuckled herself from the cockpit and looked around for help. Phil sprang to her aid like a star-struck football supporter asked to carry the boots of Europe's top striker. Later she joined us for a drink in the clubhouse and told us all about aerobatics – how she would perform at airshows. 'What you saw there was a very bad display,' she said to an utterly unconvinced circle of admirers. 'I would have scored pretty low points if that had been a competition.'

Phil was beaming like a schoolboy, probing her with questions about reverse inside back-to-back Doberman turns, or something. 'As soon as the course is over I'm going up with Josef,' he vowed. 'I want to fly upside-down. Ordinary gliding's for wimps.'

The blonde aerobat excused herself politely and left. Here was a star and yet she had been so willing to spend some time with a bunch of novices. Phil was smitten. We retired to the video-room and watched

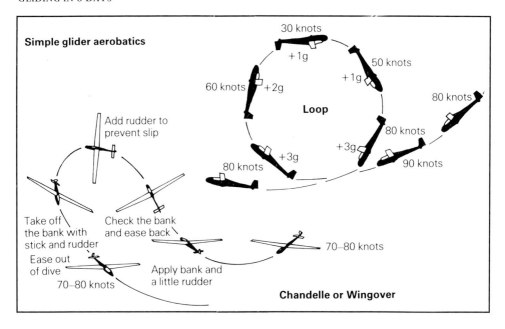

Simple glider aerobatics

30 knots

+1g

50 knots

+1g

60 knots +2g

Loop

80 knots

Add rudder to
prevent slip

80 knots

+3g

+3g

80 knots

90 knots

80 knots

Take off
the bank with
stick and rudder

Check the bank
and ease back

Ease out
of dive

70–80 knots

70–80 knots

Apply bank and
a little rudder

Chandelle or Wingover

Simple aerobatics are possible even in training gliders, but the real stunts are best left to the professionals like Hilary.

the second half of *The Blue Max*, a film set in France during the First World War about the rise and fall (literally) of a young German flying officer.

George Peppard was sneering down the sights of his twin machine-gins. G, drawn from the bar to the video-room by the sound of three of his dedicated glider pilots in a spirited chorus of '*dakadakadaka-daka*', poked his nose round the door. 'We're getting some flying tips from Derek Piggott,' said Phil, quick as a flash as Piggott doubled for Baron von Richtofen at the controls of a Fokker triplane at that precise moment on screen. G retired with a sigh. We had already devoured most of Lasham's library of gliding videos and the film was damn good. Besides, we were relaxing...

DAY EIGHT

Friday dawned clear but slightly colder than it had been. The weather, which had held up so magnificently for four days, was on the change. The windsock indicated a freshening 15-knot breeze blowing more or less straight down the runway, and if ever there was a day for breaking in the flying suit this was it.

Breakfast changed all that. As usual there was a distinct lack of the kind of dress-sense you might expect in a bunch of pilots. It was more like a works canteen or a smart roadside café. I could discern no pattern to gliding couture – and certainly no flying suits.

At that point the wind blew in a leather jacket and boots, enclosing what must have been the uninitiated's ideal of a pilot, were it not for the fact that he swung a crash helmet from its straps. 'Anyone tell me where I can find G & M Engineering?' said the flustered dispatch rider.

Slinking back to my room to change I reappeared a few minutes later wearing customary jeans, thick shirt and padded jacket. I ordered sausage, bacon, beans and tomatoes, joined the others at breakfast, hitched a ride in John's VW camper to the control van and waited my turn.

Although this was the last day I knew that there was to be no climax. There would be no fanfares for this new pilot – and absolutely no prospect of going solo. I'd been disabused of that idea early on. What I could achieve, and was determined to do, was to fly the glider from start to finish with no help from G. By now I had handled the glider single-handed in all phases of launch, flight and landing, but always at some point G had been forced to take over.

If I could only achieve one hands-on flight from beginning to end it would be enough.

My number was called just after ten o'clock. The wind, by then, was gusting to 20 knots. 'The glider's going to want to lift off much earlier with this headwind,' said G as we ran through the now familiar checks, but there was a long wait for the tug. It was unusually cool in the cockpit. 'Close the canopy – we'll do the canopy and brakes when the tug arrives.'

There was still a great deal to learn, and now G explained about canopies. 'Keep the canopy closed at all times, especially when it's windy or it will crash down, and maybe crack. It's the most common outward sign of glider damage. They cost well over a thousand pounds to replace, so we treat them with kid gloves.'

Most cracks emanate from the corners of the sliding windows. Two of Lasham's K 13s had just such stress cracks radiating from these very points. One of them had an adequate although unsightly repair using a special epoxy glue and diamond polish.

At last a buzzing noise behind us signified that our tug was about to appear. 'Brakes out, back together and locked,' I shouted above the din.

'This is your last one, isn't it?' asked G.

'No, one more,' I replied.

After all the anticipation and despite this being my

Effect of the wind gradient

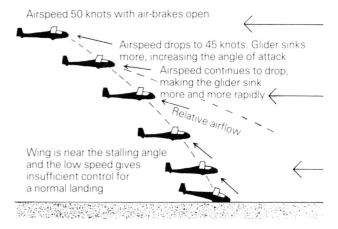

Airspeed 50 knots with air-brakes open

Airspeed drops to 45 knots. Glider sinks more, increasing the angle of attack

Airspeed continues to drop, making the glider sink more and more rapidly

Relative airflow

Wing is near the stalling angle and the low speed gives insufficient control for a normal landing

At one moment a glider can be flying into a 30-knot wind, but due to the slowing effect as the wind passes over the ground, a few feet lower and the glider may be semi-stalled, with the obvious dangers.

last day, the dénouement was curiously anti-climatic. There is very little to say about that 18th flight. We did, in fact, lift off early as the headwind took us. The combination of the tug's forward speed, about 65 knots, and the 20-knot wind, which rose as we climbed through the wind gradient, meant that our ground-speed was perhaps only 45 knots, but we were in the air within seconds. I thought I detected G's steadying hand on the controls as we swept through 1,500 feet but no – he swore that he hadn't touched a thing. We circled for about eight minutes in complete silence. Not once did I hear those heart-sinking words 'I *have it*' from behind. From aerotow to landing the glider was mine. G was the navigator and adviser – no more, no less.

My last flight of the day was similarly silent. By mid-morning the wind was on the limit for safe flying and G was being extra careful about making sure the gliders were parked wings down into the wind, with plenty of tyres to stop them flipping. The windsock was streaming near horizontal as I waited in the cockpit for the tug that was take me on my last flight of the course.

Again we were airborne within seconds. Despite the strength of the wind, which increased as we climbed, the air was smooth and turbulence-free and again, without prompting, I flew the glider without help. Moreover I felt more relaxed than ever. Not only

Airfield activity centres around the bus where pilots wait their turn to be towed into (what looks like here) a good thermalling sky. Behind them a line of gliders wait their turn for the winch. The trailer contains medical supplies in case of emergencies – although sunburn is by far the biggest danger in gliding.

did I have the controls, but felt completely in control. The entries in my log-book were short and to the point:

Flight 18. ASK 13 Lasham AT P2 11 All a/t. Good handling, approaches and landings.

Flight 19. ASK 13 Lasham AT P2 15 Very windy conditions. Good progress.

But what, exactly, did 'good progress' mean? The break in my career between Booker and Lasham probably hindered things by a day or so and realistically there was no way I could have hoped to be flying alone after just 19 flights, but was I ever going to be any good? I had achieved about all I was naturally capable of in the time available – but average or above average, who knows? As we broke for lunch I asked G to tell me straight: 'Would I make a pilot?' That evening he filed his end of term report. 'Be honest,' I'd said. And here, in its unexpurgated version, is what he wrote:

'You've now got a good idea of how to handle the glider, how to fly straight, turn gently or tightly, how to control the speed, how to use the air-brakes and how to land.

All these things came fairly quickly with no problems, other than a tendency to move the controls around jerkily. Remember to be very smooth – think ahead and you don't have to shove the controls about. After all, you don't twitch the controls around on your bike – fly in the same way.

Also remember to look out frequently and systematically – it's always hard to appreciate how important this is. Looking out is <u>vital</u>.

Next comes judgement. Learning how to fly a circuit, how to ensure you land in an appropriate place and learning to deal with emergency situations. We haven't started this part of flying yet – it's a good idea to be really confident in the general handling before being expected to <u>think</u> as well as fly.

You've got the potential to fly well – brain is reasonably switched on and co-ordination and perception are good. If you really want to be a top-class pilot you have to fall in love with flying – just treating it as a hobby doesn't get you anywhere. It's very expensive in terms of time and commitment and incredibly frustrating – these things take their toll.

In short, you could learn to be good at it – so how much do you want to do it?'

That was a good question. The drop-out rate in gliding is high. So many things happen to sidetrack even the keenest glider pilot – marriage, children, work, just time. In order to keep the club running and replenish the supply of pilots, Lasham has to train well over 200 a year, over half of whom never return. Once the course is finished most people seem satisfied and, perhaps despite their best intentions, leave it at that. The longer they leave it, the harder it is to get back into the habit of gliding. Would I be the exception? And what would it be like without the calm G in the back?

To find out I decided to stay on that weekend, if only for one flight. There were photos to take and my old friend Jason, who had not flown since New Zealand, had promised to come down for a couple of flights. What would they make of his experience? Would the cautious instructors at Lasham unleash him over Hampshire on his own on the strength of a few solo flights two years ago in Australia?

As it happened the answer was an emphatic 'No', which cheered me in a malicious sort of way. We were level pegging again.

––––––

With G off flying his Jantar, no doubt glad to be rid of students for a couple of days, we were at the mercy of Lasham's weekend instructors, one of the 90 qualified to take students, and like debs at a ball we signed our names and waited to be invited to dance. Eventually we were approached by a tallish man in his late thirties, who spoke with an unmistakeable Scottish accent. 'Who's next?' inquired Nigel Maclean.

Jason, never the shrinking violet, shoved his log-book out and began to explain he was an experienced solo pilot. Ten minutes later I watched the K 13 make its jerky way into the blue sky. When they were safely down Jason told me how it had gone. 'They're a lot more fussy over here, but he says I'll be able to go up this afternoon – perhaps.'

Nigel didn't appear so sure, at least to me. 'He's good, but a little over-confident, but don't tell him. He's a bit rusty, but that's not surprising. He'll be solo within a few more flights, no problem. And how about you?'

Nigel seemed calm and reassuring. 'So, what have you done so far?' he asked, taking my log-book. 'Nineteen flights. I see you've got a good idea of aerotowing. Turning seems to be coming along. How about stalls and incips? Maybe we'll do some of those and just see how long we can keep up there.'

'I tend to lose it in a big way on aerotow,' I said, not untruthfully.

'Thanks for telling me,' responded Nigel. 'I'll watch it.'

'Boxing the wake' is an exercise in aerotow control that entails flying high, low and to the side of the tug's wake.

I detected a trace of concern, but my warning was groundless. He had nothing to fear. The aerotow was perfect. We even had time to practise what's called 'boxing the wake' – taking up a position in turns below and to either side of the tug before resuming the normal high tow position, where the tug is just above the horizon.

At 2,000 feet I released. Dodging the tow rope with a hesitant left bank we were immediately in a thermal. 'Go right, now!' said the voice from the back, urgently.

I wasn't used to this. The voice was brusque, impatient even, unlike G. The difference was simple. This, my third 'voice in the back', was that of a man who was first and foremost a pilot, not an instructor. 'Steeper, level out. Damn, we've lost it. OK, bank right again. Now! That's better!' The altimeter was climbing slowly again. The vario showed about three knots of lift.

Just as suddenly the lift had turned to sink. We'd been flying at a steady 45 knots until then. Instinctively I brought the stick back thinking that the slower we were to go, the less neight we would lose.

'No!' said the voice from behind. 'Always *increase* the speed when you fly into sink. Get through it as fast as you can. There's no point hanging around in sink. Get to the next thermal as quickly as possible with the minimum height loss.'

This was puzzling, to say the least. In all the flights thus far I'd never been sufficiently aware of the significance of sink. Now that we were trying our utmost to prolong flight, I instinctively sought to slow the glider, hoping to keep us up longer.

The reaction to slow down is a natural one, just as it is when you approach a landing into a strong headwind. The brain thinks 'the slower I go, the less height I'll use up'. In both cases, landing into strong winds and in heavy sink, the glider must be flown faster than normal. *Think*, Morgan.

No longer was I just controlling the glider, but also trying to keep it up. Quite understandably, Nigel was teaching me how to feel the presence of thermals. Without that knowledge much of what had been learnt would be wasted.

'Look out ahead and you'll see a fluffy white cloud beginning to form just to the right of the nose. Let's go and see if there's any lift. As you get near the cloud you'll probably notice the glider bump about like you're going over cobblestones. You may even feel the glider beginning to tip. If you feel it tipping you'll want to turn against the tipping. It means there's extra lift under one wing. If it tips to the left you'll want to go right. Here's the turbulence. Now, look round and get into the turn quickly.'

We then circled, trying to get into the centre of lift. The vario was rising. As we came round the turn we

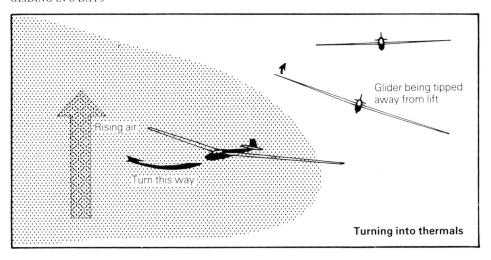

Rising air

Turn this way

Glider being tipped
away from lift

Turning into thermals

The classic signs of thermal presence is the wing-tip lifting as it enters the rising air. The pilot must be alert to this and bank towards the lift without delay.

straightened up and went into the same turn, well banked and steady at about 45 knots.

Clouds form above thermals. The sun heats up the ground unevenly and also evaporates moisture – dew in the early morning and later moisture from the crops. When the thermal leaves the ground as a bubble of air it contains some invisible water vapour. As it goes up the air expands and cools. Eventually the moisture saturates the air and condenses out at a certain height because cool air does not hold as much moisture as warm air. Cumulus clouds form. If the air lifts gradually over mountains, or if the air blows out over the sea, for example, you get layers of cloud, which is no good. Cumulus is an indication that there is, or has been, a thermal.

Cumulus starts with a little patch of haze. Then the haze begins to form into a cloud and gets bigger. Eventually the air surrounding the clouds is all drier than the cloud, so the cloud begins to evaporate, gets stragglier where it evaporates and cools as it goes down. The life of a small cloud may only be ten minutes. Larger clouds may be kept fed by more thermals. Some clouds are flat, even hollow, but the darker the base the more indication that the cloud is solid. If it's evaporating you can usually see some sunlight filtering through. The idea is to pick the clouds that are developing, rather than decaying.

Steep turns normally lose height, but they pay in strong thermals as you can remain in the centre of lift. The first turn is usually a tight one until you know whether you are in the best lift.

Hill lift, where the wind blows up the side, is more limited, usually only twice the height of the ridge.

Wave lift is set up by the mountains and occurs at Lasham very rarely as a result of oscillations built up many miles away to the north-west. When the conditions are right wave lift can extend right up to the stratosphere, 30,000 feet or more. It's rather like having an invisible hill beneath you.

———

During the next 15 minutes or so I was made to do more turns in a shorter time than ever before. I had little if any time to think, just a quick lookout and then – bang, into the turn, watching the wing-tips scoring the fields below, then back level and hard left again, almost before I realised what was happening.

The airfield could have been anywhere. I had no idea where we were. I hoped Nigel did.

Next we tried stalling. This time I was made to bring the nose up, feeling the shaking, feeding out the wing drop into a smooth forward stick movement; as the glider flung itself earthwards before dragging skywards again with a rush that sent the airspeed indicator scurrying round the dial, the 'g forces' pressed my body to the seat.

As we pulled out of an incipient spin, Nigel pointed towards the airfield, lower than usual to our left. This wasn't what I had expected. Normally after our exercises G had somehow contrived to leave us heading downwind for the final turn.

Instead we were heading into wind, gaining only fractionally against the ground. 'When do you think we should turn, then?' said Nigel, a little urgently. I looked at the altitude. 'We've got a thousand feet at the moment. I think we should go anyway.'

Final turns should be well banked, decisive and with the speed well controlled for a perfect landing in the chosen place.

Final turns

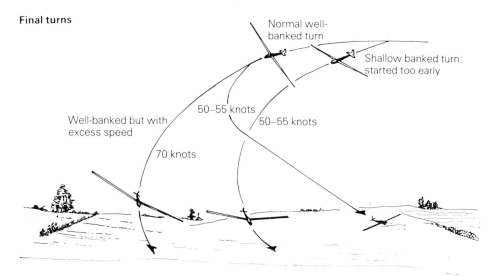

Normal well-banked turn

Shallow banked turn: started too early

50–55 knots

50–55 knots

Well-banked but with excess speed

70 knots

'I've got seven hundred back here,' said Nigel. 'That's low. Tap your altimeter.'

I did, and the needle flicked down 300 feet. 'Christ, you're right! Let's go!'

'Go now and make it tight,' said Nigel. 'We're running out of height fast.'

Nigel had every right to sound alarmed. I'd been flying carelessly, safe in the knowledge that he could always take over if necessary. While that was true for a manoeuvre that had gone wrong, there's nothing an instructor can do if the glider is too low other than attempt to land upfield as quickly as possible. The sense that I was responsible for the flight had never been as strong. There was no immediate danger, but I'd allowed myself to be lulled into a false sense of security. I'd been so involved in thermalling that I'd ignored the fundamental lesson: always be aware of where you are in relation to the field, and watch your instruments.

After the mental exertion of the previous ten minutes, the expected brief respite before having to think about the landing would have been welcome. There was to be none. I had to think as if I were on my own. It was windy and the glider was already a little low. We would have to turn into the approach faster and tighter than ever before to prevent undershooting. To cap it all there was a sudden groan from the back. 'It's OK. I've just got cramp in my foot. I can't move it off the pedals.' There was an agonised shuffling as Nigel tried to massage some feeling back into his protesting limb. 'It's better, but I won't be able to help you out for a sec if you get out of shape'.

'Great,' I thought, trying not to think about that film where the pilot gets food poisoning.

I threw the glider into a steep left bank, dabbing the rudder as we went, then straightened up and watched the airfield slip faster and faster away behind the right wing. It must have been blowing a good 35 knots up there. That meant the airfield was 'moving' at nearly 90 knots.

The end of the runway was approaching fast. Soon it would be abreast and, if we did not make a smooth and efficient final turn, we'd be clawing for height over the spiky green stuff beyond the perimeter. What's more, there was bound to be sink over the trees. Before long we'd be into the low and probably slow syndrome.

I turned early, anticipating Nigel's call – a little too early, perhaps, but in a strong headwind and with a potential height problem that's no bad thing. The worst that can happen is that the glider will fetch up at

Ballooning

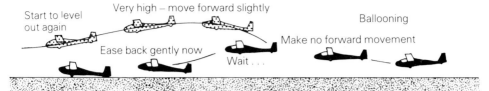

Start to level out again

Very high – move forward slightly

Ballooning

Make no forward movement

Ease back gently now

Wait . . .

Holding off too high

Now ease back gently

Holding off too high

Wait . . .

the top end of the field, but that's infinitely better than landing in the trees or pitching into the perimeter.

'Make it a steep one,' said Nigel as the right wing-tip dropped into the field. 'Half air-brakes. We're a little too high after all that.'

I blew the landing checks completely. All I could remember was 'Is there anything loose floating around the cockpit? Um ... that's it.' There wasn't time. The combination of air-brake and steep turn had brought us up perfectly placed to see the airfield spread out in front. Airspeed was a good 55 knots. I gave the glider full air-brakes for a second and the aiming point, a line about 30 years into the runway, began to recede over the nose. We were undershooting. Easing the air-brakes back to half the aiming point steadied, and the glider bellied in towards the grass. I rounded out a little early – maybe three 'elephants' – and let the glider settle down of its own accord. There was a bump, the grass swam towards us and we came to a gentle stop 50 yards from the control bus, bang opposite the line of gliders waiting for an aerotow.

'That was a bit hairy,' I said. 'It all happened so fast and I've never done a complete circuit planning before. Did you really get cramp, Nigel, or was that just a ploy?'

'No, really, it was just a twinge,' protested the instructor. 'You probably felt me trying to straighten my leg through the rudder pedals. You did well. A little, how shall I say, rushed, perhaps – but good.'

And that was that. No prize-giving, no speeches and definitely no laurels. Nigel took my log-book,

Ballooning is a common fault, but easily corrected if the stick is held steady and the glider allowed to sink in its own good time. If the ballooning happens very high the glider may be eased forward slightly. Holding off too high also entails having a little patience: sooner or later Holding off too high also what's gone up will come down.

Six months later the author pretends that he's just gone solo . . .

flipped to the second page and wrote in what seemed rather shaky handwriting a few brief words about the flight. The words '*very good*' appeared, the rest was to the point. The next man who read those words would want facts, not generalities.

———

As I walked the field towards the life of nine-to-five my elation was mixed with sadness. Sad that it was all over, but elated that I'd achieved a personal goal and, to my amazement, conquered that fear of flying. Now there was no turning back, no way was I going to let this new-found addiction to flight grow cold. My log-book held the brief outline of just 20 flights, but it was a start. I resolved there and then to be flying solo before that second page had been exhausted. And I'd save the flying suit for that moment, whenever that would be.

It would in fact be just a matter of months. A piece of cake, really . . .

GLOSSARY

ADVERSE YAW If the glider is banked using ailerons alone, without the rudder, the nose swings away from the direction turn due to aileron drag.

AILERON The control surfaces on the trailing edges of the wings that cause the gilder to bank when the stick is moved laterally.

AILERON DRAG The price paid for the lift gained in one wing when the aileron is depressed, and which is counteracted by a small opposite movement on the rudder.

AIR-BRAKES Spoilers on the wings that reduce the wing's lift and which can be opened to enable the pilot to burn off excess height and control the approach angle and speed, usually on the final approach.

AEROTOW Launching method where the glider is towed to the required height behind a light aircraft, as opposed to a winch tow.

AIMING POINT The reference point on the ground at which the glider's nose is pointed in the final approach under or over which the glider will shoot

depending on how much, or little, air-brake is open.

ANGLE OF ATTACK The angle at which the glider's wings meet the oncoming airflow. Too great an angle of attack will eventually cause the glider to stall, at which point the stick is moved forward to allow the glider to pick up speed and 'unstall' itself.

BASE LEG The portion of the landing sequence, across the wind in a conventional into-wind landing, before the final turn is made and the glider lined up for the final approach.

BALLOONING The tendency for the glider to rise up a few feet from the ground on the final approach if the speed is too high and the pilot rounds out too soon with too much backward movement on the stick. The glider is, basically, trying to climb again.

BLUE DAYS Days on which the absence of clouds indicates an absence of thermal activity and consequently a bad day for soaring.

CB SIFT CB Pilot checks before launching: Controls, Ballast, Straps,

Instruments, Flaps, Trim, Canopy, Brakes.

CIRCUIT PLANNING The decisions taken by the glider pilot prior to landing. This consists of when and at what height, depending on conditions, to turn for the downwind leg, leading to the base leg and final approach.

CROSSWIND A wind that blows across the landing area.

CUMULUS The cloud most usually associated with thermals. The presence of cumulus indicates that a thermal is working or has just stopped working.

DOWNWIND LEG The first component of the landing procedure when the glider is flown downwind, to one side of the runway, before turning across the wind (base leg) and then into the wind for the final approach.

DRAG The force that stops any object gaining speed infinitely as it falls through the air. Drag is minimised by having smooth surfaces with as few as possible protruberances. Gliders are very susceptible to drag and, for that reason, great care is taken to keep them clean.

ELEVATOR The control surface on the tail that allows the pilot to alter the pitch of the glider, thus increasing or decreasing speed.

FULL SPIN A downward, near-vertical spiral in which the wings are stalled.

GLIDING ANGLE The distance the glider will sink for every foot it flies forward. Some high-performance gliders have a gliding angle of 50:1, which means that in level flight they will sink only one foot for every 50 feet they travel forwards. Most gliders have a gliding angle of 16-35:1. Hang gliders have a gliding angle of about 10:1.

GRADIENT EFFECT The reduction in wind-speed with height due to the slowing of the wind, caused by friction as it passes over the ground.

HOLD OFF The technique where the pilot allows the glider to land itself, rather than fly it into the ground by keeping the stick held back on the final part of the landing.

ROUND OUT The penultimate stage of the final approach when the glider's nose is levelled off at about five feet.

INCIPIENT SPINS The start of a full spin when one or other of the wings has stalled and begins to drop – which, unless corrected, will lead to a full spin.

PILOT INDUCED OSCILLATION A common beginner's fault where the pilot continues to overcorrect on the controls and starts to exaggerate rather than damp out any slight pitching or yawing.

PITCH The vertical movement of the glider up and down, controlled by the elevator.

RIDGE LIFT The effect of wind meeting a hill that causes an updraught which can be used for soaring.

RUDDER The control surface on the tail that controls the glider's yaw, used sparingly in the turns to counteract aileron drag.

SIDE SLIPPING The effect of too little rudder in a turn which causes the fuselage to take up an angle with the airflow, rather than meet it head on. The opposite is a skidding turn, when too much rudder is applied.

SINK An air mass that is sinking – as opposed to lift, which is encountered in thermals.

SOARING Flight that takes place in lift. Soaring flights of five hours or more can be made in good conditions, using pockets of lift, or thermals, to counter-act every glider's tendency to sink.

SPIN When the glider's wings have stalled completely. Spins are easily counteracted by opposite rudder and moving forward on the stick until the glider unstalls, when the wings regain lift and control is regained.

STALL/STALLING POINT The point at which the wings lose their lift and can no longer support the weight of the glider and pilot.

THERMALS Rising air, usually due to the warming effect of the sun on the ground, which causes moist air to rise and condense out into cumulus clouds.

TRIM The attitude the glider takes up naturally if the controls are left alone. Trim can be altered by moving the trim tab on the elevator to counteract the tendency of the glider to pivot around its centre of gravity.

YAW The side-to-side component of flight, controlled by the rudder.

YAW STRING A short length of yarn attached to the outside of the canopy that indicates whether the fuselage is meeting the airflow head on, which is efficient, or at an angle, especially in a turn – ie slipping or skidding.

APPENDIX

FURTHER READING

Books

Beginning Gliding
The Fundamentals of Soaring
Derek Piggott
(A & C Black)

Understanding Gliding: The Principles of Soaring Flight
Derek Piggott
(A & C Black)

Going Solo: A Simple Guide to Soaring
Derek Piggott
(A & C Black)

Gliding (5th Edition): A Handbook of Soaring Flight
Derek Piggott
(A & C Black)

Understanding Flying Weather
Derek Piggott
(A & C Black)

Meterology and Flight: A Pilot's Guide to Weather
Tom Bradbury
(A & C Black)

Happy to Fly
Anne Welch

Gliding Competitively
John Dellafield
(A & C Black)

Soaring Across Country
Bill Scull
(Pelham)

Adventures of a Half-baked Chicken-hearted Granny Glider Pilot
Mary Meagher
(Ava Books)

Elementary Gliding
(British Gliding Association)

Laws and Rules
(British Gliding Association)

Periodicals

Sailplane and Gliding (UK)
Soaring (US)